"Tell Them All About It, Won't You?"

Images of the Present, Voices of the Past
Gettysburg

Photographs by Helen S. Schwartz
Text by Katharine A. Sloan
Edited by Kristin D. Murray
Formatting by Alex MacDonald

Published by Artistry in Photography
P.O. Box 491
Langhorne, PA 19047

Title quoted in *The Sixteenth Maine Regiment in the War of the Rebellion 1861-1865* by Major A.R. Small, p. 128

Front cover photo, The Field at the Angle
Back cover photo, 116th Pennsylvania Infantry Monument on Sickles Ave

Photographs © 2006 Helen S. Schwartz
All Photographs are sole property of Helen S. Schwartz
All Rights Reserved

This book may not be reproduced, translated or transmitted, photographs or text (except the quotes), in whole or in part, in any form or by any means, electronic or mechanical including photocopying, recording or by any information storage and retrieval system now known or hereafter invented without written permission from Helen S. Schwartz. All Rights Reserved.

ISBN 0-9776959-1-3

Published by Artistry in Photography
    P.O. Box 491
    Langhorne, PA 19047
    e-mail- HSSAIP@comcast.net
    website- www.artistryinphotography.com

PRINTED IN THE UNITED STATES OF AMERICA

For Julian & Max,
The next generation to fall in love with Gettysburg

Acknowledgments

There are a number of folks we'd like to thank for helping us along in this venture. With gratitude and respect, we acknowledge the contributions of the men & women, soldiers & civilians, Union & Confederate who struggled and suffered through the events of July 1863.

Helen thanks: My inner guidance. My family and friends for their love and support, with special mention of Dad and Jan. I would like to thank Mom, Lois and Jerry Skoff. Kathy Sloan for her friendship and beautiful writing, and for bringing me to Gettysburg for the first time. Bernadette Loeffel Atkins for her encouragement and for writing the foreword in this book. The many Park Rangers, Tour Guides and Historians who have inspired and educated me. Paul and Rosemarie Lafollette; Nancy Russell and, in memoriam, Jim Russell; Michelle McCarthy, Stevan J. Thayer and IET®; Jacob Schwartz, Kristin Murray, Cheryl Kelly, Ryan Gillespie — Webmaster, Cousin Judith, Garry Starrett, Jr., Becky Murphy, Albert Cook, Donna Trout; Alex MacDonald for being a trusted friend and for making our projects possible....and most of all, Gail Kehler; my dear friend who urged me to share my work, created Artistry in Photography with me, and for her continuing trust, friendship and support artistically and in Business Management.

Kathy would like to thank: her sister Peg, brothers Tim, Bob, Bill, John & Joe; her niece, Stephanie and Steph's husband John, who are both lovers of Gettysburg (and thank you for Max, the next generation!); her nephew Brian who is a positive force in the world; also our friend Donna (who was freezing with us on Little Round Top that first day) and thank you, Helen, for that phone call. You've helped me to live my dream.

Foreword

Approximately 2 million visitors come to Gettysburg every year. Some come for the history, others for the bucolic beauty of Adams County and many come here out of curiosity. It is on this hallowed ground that the greatest battle ever fought on the continent occurred. It was also the bloodiest single battle of the American Civil War, resulting in over 51,000 soldiers killed, wounded, captured or missing.

Today, Gettysburg National Military Park stands as one of the largest battlefield shrines in the United States. The Park incorporates nearly 6,000 acres, with 26 miles of park roads and over 1,400 monuments, memorials and markers dedicated to those brave men who fought here.

This book tells the story of these men. With the soldiers' words, the informative text of writer Katharine A. Sloan and the poignant and haunting photographs of historical landscape photographer, Helen S. Schwartz, they capture the essence that is Gettysburg, a place to meditate, reflect and learn.

Bernadette Loeffel Atkins
Gettysburg, PA
December 14, 2005

"You must be the change you wish to see in the world."
Mahatma Gandhi

Introduction

"In great deeds something abides. On great fields, something stays. Forms change and pass; bodies disappear; but spirits linger, to consecrate ground for the vision-place of souls. And reverent men and women from afar, and generations that know us not and that we know not of, heart-drawn to see where and by whom great things were suffered and done for them, shall come to this deathless field, to ponder and dream; and lo! The shadow of a mighty presence shall wrap them in its bosom, and the power of the vision pass into their souls."

General Joshua Lawrence Chamberlain
October 3, 1889
Quoted in *Maine at Gettysburg: Report of Maine Commissioners Prepared by the Executive Committee*,
pp. 558-559.

On a bitterly cold November day in 1993, three women stood at the crest of Little Round Top, their coats wrapped tightly around them, the wind stinging like shards of broken glass on their faces and hands. But in each of their minds rose a hot July day, the acrid smell of gunpowder burning their nostrils while the sounds of battle raged all around them. We heard the brisk orders, the clank of metal on metal, the strangled cries of the wounded and dying. It was the first time any of us had come to Gettysburg, but it would not be the last.

The "power of the vision" of which General Chamberlain had so eloquently spoken in 1889 still possesses the hills and valleys of Gettysburg and that vision still awaits an eager soul to which it can tell its story. An open heart can learn much in the peaceful silence of the battlefield. We walk along the still paths and listen with our souls and hearts for the echoes of battles won and lost, for the men and women whose lives were inexorably changed by the events of July 1863.

Inspired by "the shadow of a mighty presence," Helen began to take achingly beautiful photographs, capturing the soul of the battlefield and allowing others to be drawn into the terrible splendor that lives there. Sitting on the crest of Little Round Top and watching the sun pass behind the Pennsylvania hills, Kathy began to empty her heart onto the page and her desire to share the poetry of valor, sacrifice and heartache was born.

It was Gail Kehler who, in 2002, suggested that Helen sell her photographs and together they formed the company, Artistry in Photography. While exhibiting in an art show in Gettysburg, Helen and Gail presented a box of note cards with Helen's images of Gettysburg Battlefield on them to the bookstore manager, Bernadette Loeffel Atkins. Bernadette suggested that they put educational text on them and submit the cards for review. Helen almost immediately telephoned Kathy and the seed of this book was planted. We have been selling note cards, matted, and framed prints for a few years now and this book is a collection of those efforts.

You'll notice, as you go along, that the photographs are not in the order of battle. We have done this intentionally. It is our intent to capture you visually and emotionally and in the hope that you'll be inspired to learn more.

Our nation's history is a rare and precious thing. Preservation is the greatest honor our generation can offer to the men who struggled here and the best gift we can leave to future generations. We urge you to support the efforts to preserve the battlefields here at Gettysburg and elsewhere in our glorious country.

We hope you enjoy our work, but more than that, we hope we'll help to fulfill Will Jenkins' dying request of Abner Small; that we can, in some small way, "Tell them all about it."

Helen S. Schwartz
Katharine A. Sloan
Gail Kehler

The Field at the Angle

"'Will you see your color storm the wall alone?' One man only starts to follow. Almost half way to the wall, down go color bearer and color to the ground; the gallant sergeant is dead. The line springs. The crest of the solid ground, with a great roar, heaves forward its maddened load – men, arms, smoke, fire, a fighting mass. It rolls to the wall. Flash meets flash. The wall is crossed. A moment ensues of thrusts, yells, blows, shots and undistinguishable conflict, followed by a shout, universal, that makes the welkin ring again; and the last and bloodiest fight of the great battle of Gettysburg is ended and won."

Lt. Frank A. Haskell
Aide-de-Camp to General John Gibbon
Quoted in *Gettysburg* by Lt. Frank A. Haskell and Col. William C. Oates, p. 224

Now only a soft golden field, illuminated by the last rays of an autumn sun, here is the Angle, where the Confederate army broke upon the wall of Union resistance. On July 3, 1863, this field was covered in the bodies of men and horses. While we may make the nearly mile long hike from the Virginia Memorial to this spot and muse on what it was like to be there that day, we may be grateful that we will never really know.

3rd Maryland Infantry/McDougall's Brigade

"It was the most fearful fire I ever encountered and my heart was sickened with the sight of so many gallant men sacrificed."

Lieutenant Randolph McKim
Staff Officer to Gen. George Steuart, CSA
Quoted in *Gettysburg: Day Three* by Jeffrey D. Wert, p. 85.

Sunlight dances at the base of Culp's Hill, illuminating the marker for Col. Archibald McDougall's First Brigade. Although this particular brigade did not see much of the fighting on Culp's Hill, the battle at the top of the hill was deadly. The Confederates assaulted the hill on the evening of July 2nd and were repulsed by a tenacious Union brigade lead by Brigadier General George S. Greene. The next morning the Confederates tried again and were once more driven off by now reinforced Union troops. The loss for the Rebels was severe and added to the misery for the Southern cause that was July 3, 1863.

The Tree at the Angle

"But Webb's men, with their bodies in part protected by the abruptness of the crest, now sent back in the enemy's faces as fierce a storm. Some scores of venturesome Rebels that in their first push at the wall had dared to cross at the further angle, and those that had desecrated Cushing's guns, were promptly shot down, and speedy death met him who should raise his body to cross it again."

Frank A. Haskell
Aide-de-camp to General John Gibbon
Quoted in *Gettysburg* by Lt. Frank A. Haskell and Col. William C. Oates, p. 218.

The great tree at the Angle seems to be reaching its bony fingers toward the bloody wall. The monument to the left of the tree is that of the 71st Pennsylvania, originally named "the California Regiment." Recruited in Philadelphia, they were the only regiment in the Union Army attributed to the Golden State. After the death of its original commander, the state of Pennsylvania reclaimed the regiment for its own and renamed it the 71st Pennsylvania. The cannon to the right is one of Alonzo Cushing's 3 inch rifles. On July 3, 1863, during Pickett's Charge, the 71st Pennsylvania helped man Cushing's guns once all the officers of the battery had been killed or wounded.

General Robert E. Lee

"I never saw troops behave more magnificently than Pickett's division of Virginians did to-day in that grand charge upon the enemy. And if they had been supported as they were to have been, — but, for some reason not yet fully explained to me, were not — we would have held the position and the day would have been ours. Too bad! Too bad!! Oh, TOO BAD!"

General Robert E. Lee
July 3, 1863
Quoted in *Robert E. Lee: A Biography* by Emory M. Thomas, p. 301.

General Robert E. Lee gazes out toward Cemetery Ridge and the field of the devastation of Pickett's Charge. Born at Stratford Hall near Richmond in 1807, Robert Edward Lee joined the Confederacy upon the secession of Virginia, declaring that he could not "raise my hand against my relatives, my children, my home." Although he led the Rebels in their fight against the Union, his courage and devotion to his men were such that he remains, to this day, one of the most beloved generals in American history.

The Triangular Field

"My God! My God, men! Your major's down; save him! Save him!"

Col. Augustus Van Horn Ellis to the 124th New York
July 2, 1863
Quoted in *History of the 124th New York* by Charles Weygant, p. 176.

An ominous mist hangs over the Triangular Field, popularly known as the most haunted spot on the battlefield. This fenced-in meadow was the deadly clearing troops needed to cross in the assault on Devil's Den. On the afternoon of July 2, 1863, the 124th New York stood at the top of the hill and poured fire into the approaching 1st Texas regiment. The Texans retreated and the New Yorkers charged down the hill. The Texans turned and launched a volley into the impetuous New Yorkers. Compounding the New Yorkers' misery was the appearance of parts of the 44th Alabama on their left, who decimated the troops with enfilade fire. In the action, the major of the 124th New York, 22-year old James Cromwell, and its colonel, Augustus Van Horne Ellis, were both killed.

Friend to Friend Monument

"Tell General Hancock for me that I have done him and done you all an injury which I shall regret [until] ... the longest day I live."

General Lewis A. Armistead to Captain Henry H. Bingham
July 3, 1863
Quoted in *Bachelder Papers* Vol. I, p. 352.

Leading his men over the stone wall at the Angle, General Armistead was shot and mortally wounded. Falling, he gave the Masonic signal for distress. As he was being carried back to a Union field hospital, Henry Bingham, a staff officer to General Winfield Scott Hancock, and also a Mason, stopped the stretcher and offered his assistance. Armistead gave him his personal effects, which Bingham delivered to General Hancock, Armistead's old friend. Armistead died at the Spangler Farm on July 5, 1863.

Willoughby Run

"We were rather enjoying the fray, when an order was given to 'fall back on Willoughby Run.' We could see no reason for this order, as the Tennesseans were keeping the 'blue boys' busy, and things seemed going pretty well for us..."

Private W. H. Moon
Color Guard, 13th Alabama Infantry
Quoted in *Morning at Willoughby Run: July 1, 1863* by Richard S. Shue, p. 133.

The scene of the gently flowing waters of Willoughby Run belies the horrific slaughter of July 1, 1863. Confederate commander Brigadier General James J. Archer's Brigade was flanked and driven back across this creek in the morning. By the afternoon, however, the tables had turned. Re-grouped and reinforced, the Confederates charged across the creek and in another bloody struggle with the Union Iron Brigade, drove the Yankees back toward the town of Gettysburg.

Louisiana State Monument

"...here we had a hand to hand fight, the Yankees on one side and we on the other side of the wall - knocked each other down with clubbed guns and bayonets."

Member of the 8th Louisiana,
"The Louisiana Tigers"
Quoted in *Gettysburg: A Testing of Courage* by Noah Andre Trudeau, p. 405.

The Louisiana Tigers consisted of the 5th through 9th Louisiana regiments, recruited mostly from the New Orleans area. The Tigers were under the command of Brigadier General Harry T. Hays and were considered to be valiant fighters. On July 1, 1863, they turned back Union troops on what is now known as Barlow Knoll, and late on July 2nd, attacked East Cemetery Hill, but were repulsed. The Louisiana monument, located along Confederate Avenue, is placed near the battle line of the Washington Artillery, also from New Orleans, who fired the signal shot to begin the artillery barrage which preceded Pickett's Charge.

The Wheatfield

"Our fire began to tell on their ranks, which were more dense than usual. We peppered them well with musketry while Randolph's battery, which was on a gentle rise in rear of us, served a dose of grape and canister every few seconds."

Private John Haley
17th Maine Volunteer Infantry
Quoted in *Rebel Yell and the Yankee Hurrah* by Ruth Silliker, ed., p. 101.

Some of the most desperate fighting during the battle of Gettysburg took place in Rose's wheat field. Battle lines raged back and forth across the field for hours. Forces under the command of Union Colonel Philippe Regis deTrobriand held off those of Confederates Brigadier General George "Tige" Anderson and Brigadier General Henry L. Benning until the rebels of Brigadier General Joseph T. Kershaw's Brigade joined the fight. The Union forces began to retreat until reinforcements from Hancock's 2nd Corps arrived. After repeated counterattacks by the determined Confederates, Union troops were eventually driven out of the Wheatfield back towards Devil's Den and the Plum Run Valley.

The North Carolina Monument

"One poor fellow, about twenty-five years of age, was shot through the body. His wants were few - 'Only a drink of water. I am so cold - so cold! Won't you cover me up?' And then his mind wandered, murmuring something about 'Dear mother. So glad 't is all over.' Then a clear sense of his condition, and would I write to his father and tell him how he died; how he loved them at home? 'Tell them all about it, won't you? Father's name is Robert Jenkins. I belong to the Seventh North Carolina troops - came from Chatham County. My name is Will-,' and tearfully I covered his face...he was some mother's darling."

Major Abner R. Small
Adjutant, 16th Maine Volunteer Infantry
Quoted in *The Sixteenth Maine Regiment in the War of the Rebellion 1861-1865* by Major A. R. Small, p. 128.

Kissed by a ray of sunlight, the North Carolina Monument seems to leap into action on a winter's day. The monument was designed by Gutzon Borglum, the sculptor of Mount Rushmore. The artist faced his monument toward the fateful copse of trees on the Union line, as if his soldiers were ready to charge one more time. A nearby monument states that one-quarter of all soldiers killed at Gettysburg were from North Carolina, all some mothers' darling sons.

Mississippi State Memorial

"No! Crowd them — we have them on the run. Move your regiments."

General William Barksdale to his officers,
July 2, 1863
Quoted in *Gettysburg: A Testing of Courage* by Noah Andre Trudeau, p. 368.

Fiercely defending his fallen comrade and his regiment's flag, a soldier of Barksdale's Brigade forever reflects the vicious fighting of July 2, 1863. The Mississippi State Memorial is positioned at the point where Barksdale's Mississippi Brigade stepped off toward the Peach Orchard. Though General Daniel Sickles' men were ready in the Peach Orchard, Barksdale's Mississippians soon overran them. The Mississippians continued to advance, but were stopped by Union forces near Plum Run, where Barksdale was mortally wounded.

The Long Walk Back

"Come, General Pickett, this has been my fight and upon my shoulders rests the blame. The men and officers of your command have written the name of Virginia as high today as it has ever been written before."

General Robert E. Lee to General George E. Pickett
July 3, 1863
Quoted in *R.E. Lee: A Biography*, Vol. I, by Douglass Southall Freeman, p. 129.

What a long walk back it must have been! The Virginia Memorial stands solemnly in the distance. Here is where the Confederate troops, bedraggled and beaten, staggered back to the safety of their former line. Legend has it that General Lee greeted his troops as they returned to tell them it had all been his fault. Encouraged, his troops rallied, but the battle of Gettysburg was over. The Confederates retreated, taking with them a wagon train of wounded 17 miles long. They would fight another day.

11th Mississippi Volunteer Infantry Monument

"Implements of war were scattered in every direction, while here & there lay horses & men in every conceivable degree of mutilation. There are perhaps few stages of suffering of which the imagination may conceive, that were not here represented."

Lieutenant Joseph R. Peel
11th Mississippi Infantry
Quoted in *Gettysburg: A Testing of Courage* by Noah Andre Trudeau, p. 425.

As if lit by the same fires of hell they had seen in 1863, the 11th Mississippi leaps into battle again. Guarding supply trains near Cashtown on July 1st and held in reserve on the 2nd, the 11th Mississippi missed most of the first two days' battles. Part of Joseph R. Davis' Brigade, the Prairie Rifles, as they called themselves, were ordered with the other Confederate troops on July 3rd to take part in Pickett's grand assault. Holding the extreme left of the Confederate line, the 11th Mississippi was devastated by the Yankee repulse of the charge. When asked what had happened to his Brigade after the assault, Joseph Davis could only point his sword upward, unable to speak.

Colonel Strong Vincent on the 83rd Pennsylvania Monument

"The line was held, but at what a cost. Throwing himself into the breach he rallied his men, but gave up his own life. Comrades and friends, that was not a bauble thrown away. In the very flower of his young manhood, full of the highest promise, with the love of a young wife filling his thought of the future with the fairest visions, proud, gentle, tender, true, he laid his gift at his country's altar."

Private Oliver Willcox Norton
Color-Bearer, 83rd Pennsylvania, speaking of Colonel Strong Vincent
Quoted in *What Death More Glorious: A Biography of General Strong Vincent* by James H. Nevins and William B. Styple, pp. 88-89.

Colonel Strong Vincent, promoted to general on his deathbed, commanded the Third Brigade of the First Division of the Fifth Corps. Vincent's Brigade, consisting of the 83rd Pennsylvania, 44th New York, 16th Michigan and 20th Maine drove back the Confederate attack on the left flank of Little Round Top on July 2, 1863. Strong Vincent was grievously wounded in the battle and died in a field hospital five days later. He was 26 years old.

Codori Farm

"General Pickett himself halted at a barn about three hundred yards from the position of the Union troops and remained there until his division was repulsed."

Colonel William C. Oates
15th Alabama Infantry
Quoted in *Gettysburg* by Lt. Frank A. Haskell and Col. William C. Oates, p. 116-117.

The beautiful red barn in the distance is part of the Codori farm, scene of brutal clashes on the battle's third day. Used by Confederates as a holding pen for Union prisoners, the barn was also a guiding point for the Confederate charge on July 3, 1863. On that final day of the battle, General George A. Pickett is said to have stood there with his aides and directed the charge against the Union troops at the Angle.

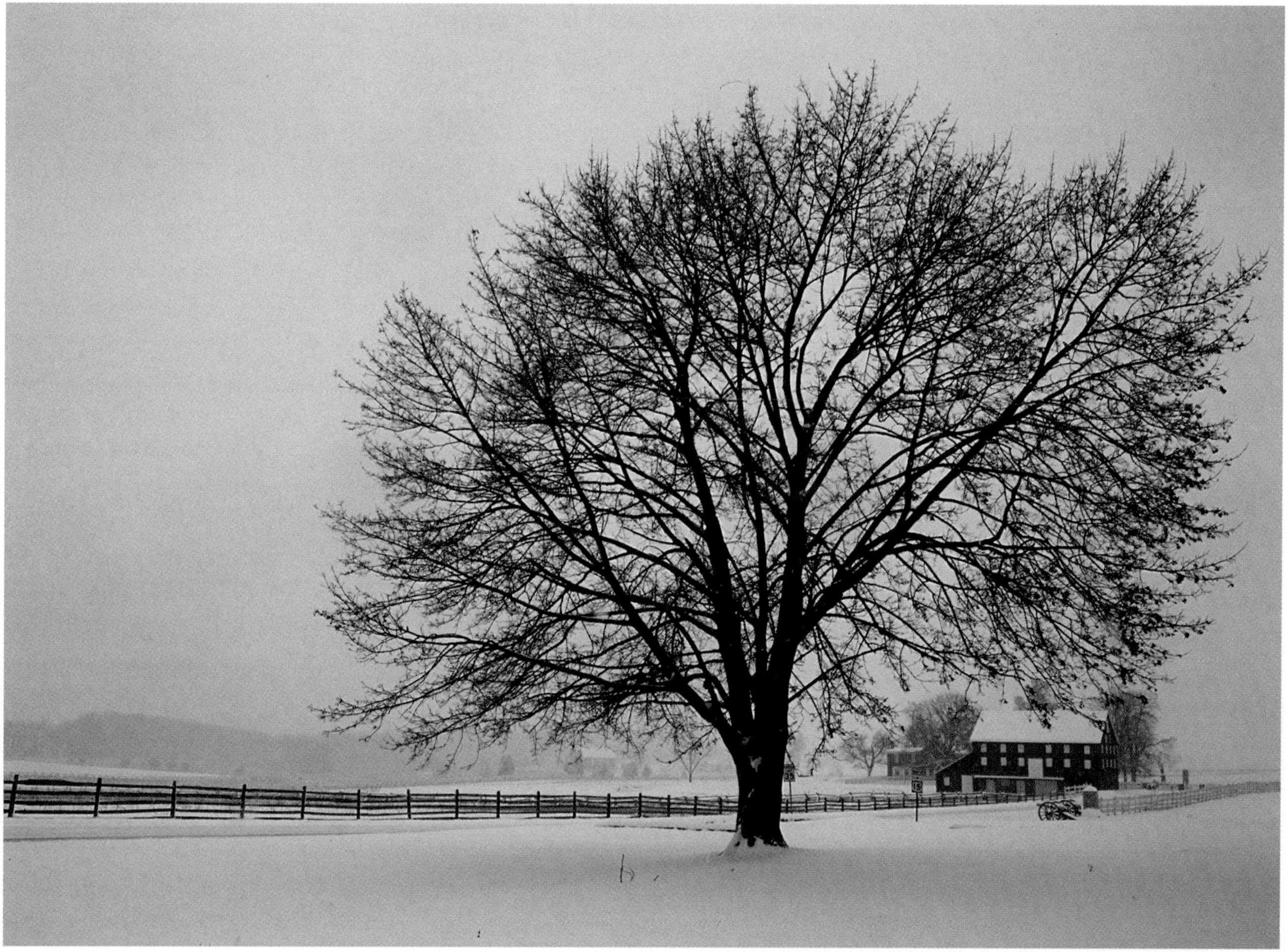

Twentieth Maine Monument

"My dead and wounded were then nearly as great in number as those still on duty. They literally covered the ground. The blood stood in puddles in some places on the rocks; the ground was soaked with the blood of as brave men as ever fell on the red field of battle."

Colonel William C. Oates
15th Alabama Infantry
Quoted in *Gettysburg* by Lt. Frank A. Haskell and Col. William C. Oates, p. 99.

Surrounded by the greenery of a soft spring day lies the monument to the 20th Maine Volunteer Infantry, commanded by Colonel Joshua Lawrence Chamberlain. On July 2, 1863, Chamberlain's 20th Maine held off a deadly assault from the 15th Alabama commanded by Colonel William C. Oates. In the hotly fought contest which raged for an intense hour, the 20th Maine emerged victorious, saving the Union left flank and earning two Medals of Honor, one for Colonel Chamberlain and the other for Sergeant Andrew Tozier, the color bearer.

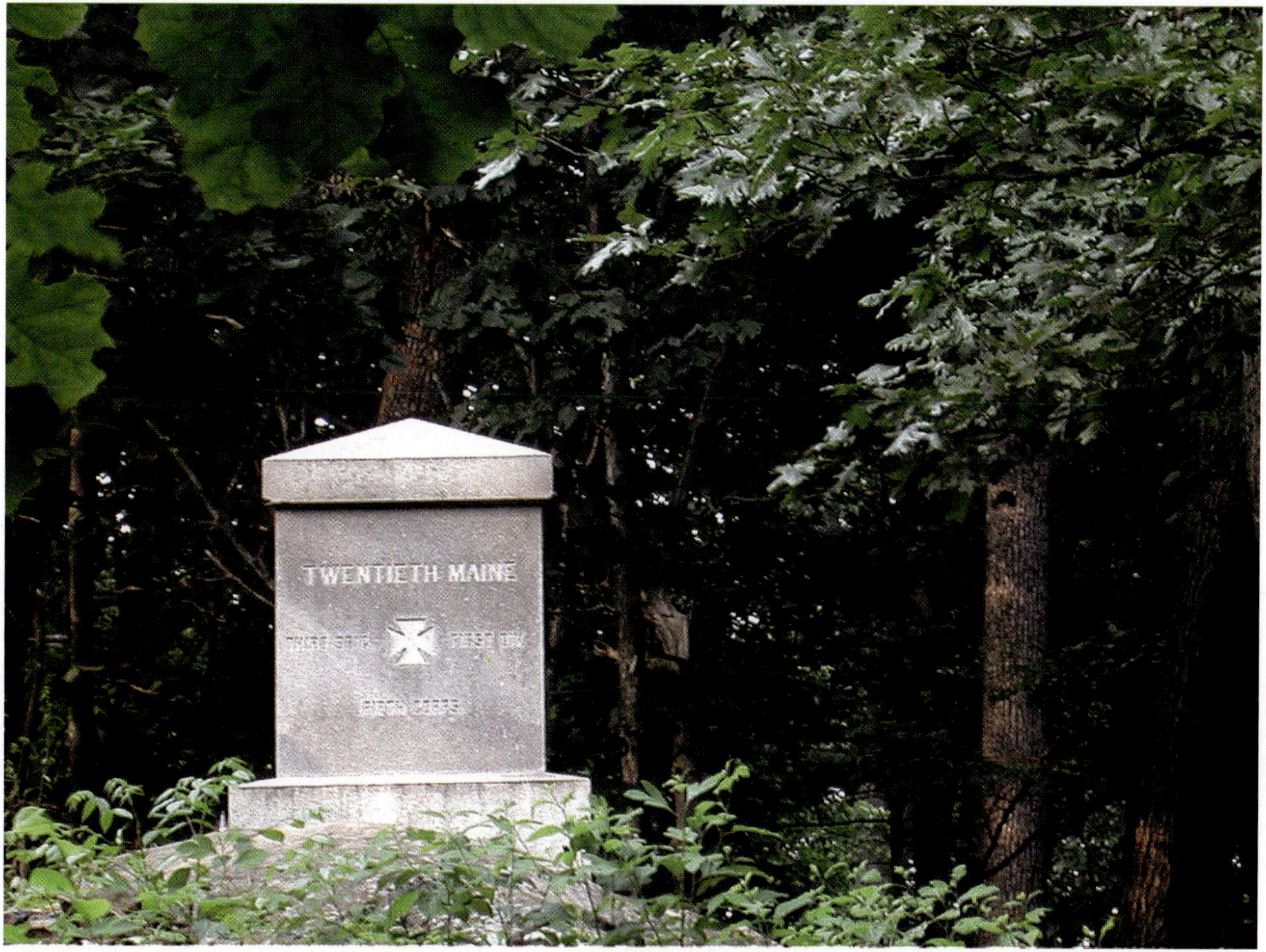
TWENTIETH MAINE

Spangler's Spring

"The oaks [formed] a grateful tent above our heads, as they had...over generations of pleasure groups; the pellucid waters of the spring [were] refreshingly cool."

Private George A. Thayer
2nd Massachusetts Volunteer Infantry
Quoted in *The Second Day at Gettysburg: Essays on Confederate and Union Leadership* by Gary W. Gallagher, ed., p. 110.

Snow and ice encrust the fountain at Spangler's Spring. Before the battle, the Spring was a popular picnic spot for local residents. During the battle, it supplied water to both sides and was the scene of repeated skirmishes between portions of the Union Twelfth Corps and Confederate Johnson's Division on the evening of July 2 and the morning of July 3, 1863.

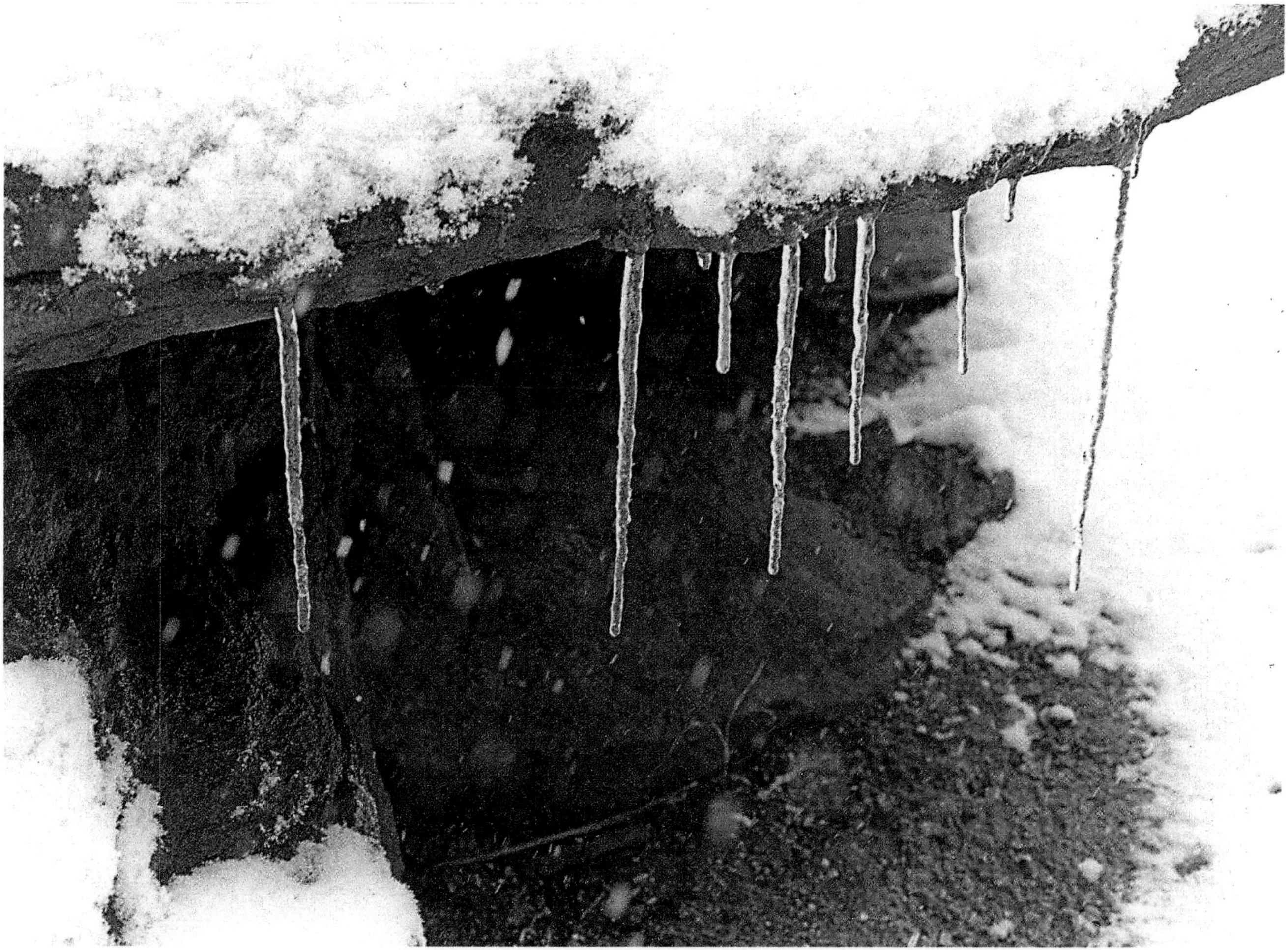

Devil's Den

"Above us then, [not] quite twenty feet, on the edge of the rock stood a line of blue coated United States regulars firing straight down at our line which had become broken in passing over and around the huge boulders which barred our way. Here fell the gallant Muse and Lieutenant Mays of my company, shot through the top of the head by the almost vertical fire. Muse fell to his left striking my feet."

Sergeant William R. Houghton
2nd Georgia Infantry
Quoted in *Devil's Den: A History and Guide* by Garry E. Adelman & Timothy H. Smith, p. 45

The huge rocks of Devil's Den were the setting for ghastly combat on July 2, 1863. The Confederates drove the Union forces from their seemingly impervious position by their overwhelming numbers. Once the Devil's Den was taken, the Confederates used the area to stage their assault on Little Round Top, some 500 yards to the east.

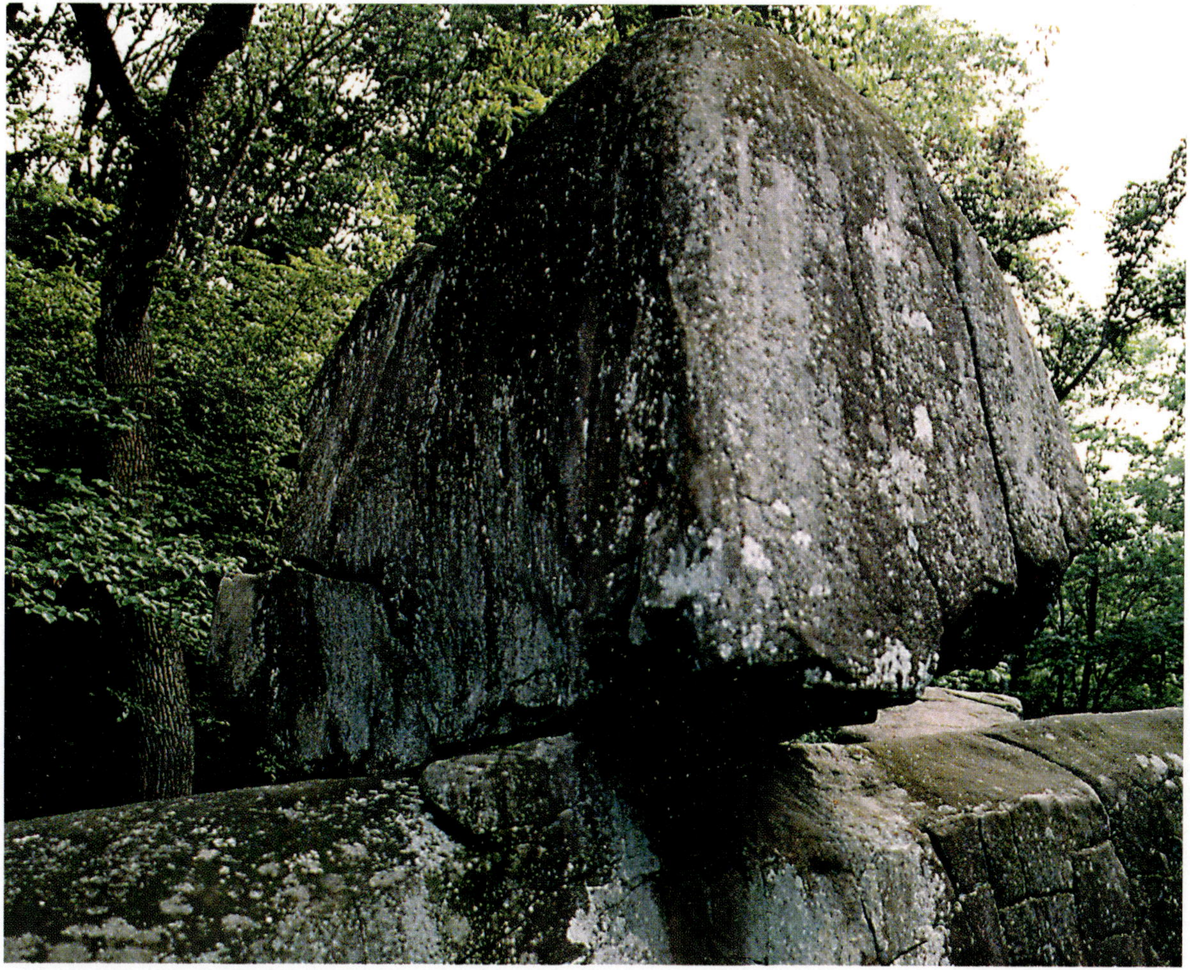

General George G. Meade

"General Meade rode up... As he arrived near me, coming up the hill, he asked in a sharp, eager voice: 'How is it going here?' 'I believe, General, the enemy's attack is repulsed,' I answered. Still approaching, and a new light began to come in his face, of gratified surprise, with a touch of incredulity, of which his voice was also the medium, he further asked: *'What, is the assault entirely repulsed?'* - his voice quicker and more eager than before. 'It is, sir,' I replied. By this time he was on the crest; and when his eye had for an instant swept over the field, taking in just a glance of the whole - the masses of prisoners; the numerous captured flags, which the men were derisively flaunting about; the fugitives of the routed enemy, disappearing with the speed of terror in the woods - partly at what I had told him, partly at what he saw, he said impressively, and his face was lighted: *'Thank God.'*"

Lieutenant Frank A. Haskell
Aide-de-Camp to General John Gibbon
Quoted in *Gettysburg* by Lt. Frank A. Haskell and Col. William C Oates, p. 229-230.

General George Gordon Meade surveys the scene of his greatest triumph. Meade was promoted to commander of the Army of the Potomac less than a week before the battle began, replacing General Joseph Hooker. Despite still adjusting to his new command, Meade took control of the army and saw it through three very difficult days. Although criticized for allowing the Confederate army to retreat over the Potomac, Meade remains the hero of the Battle, and can be credited for turning the tide of the war firmly in the Union's favor.

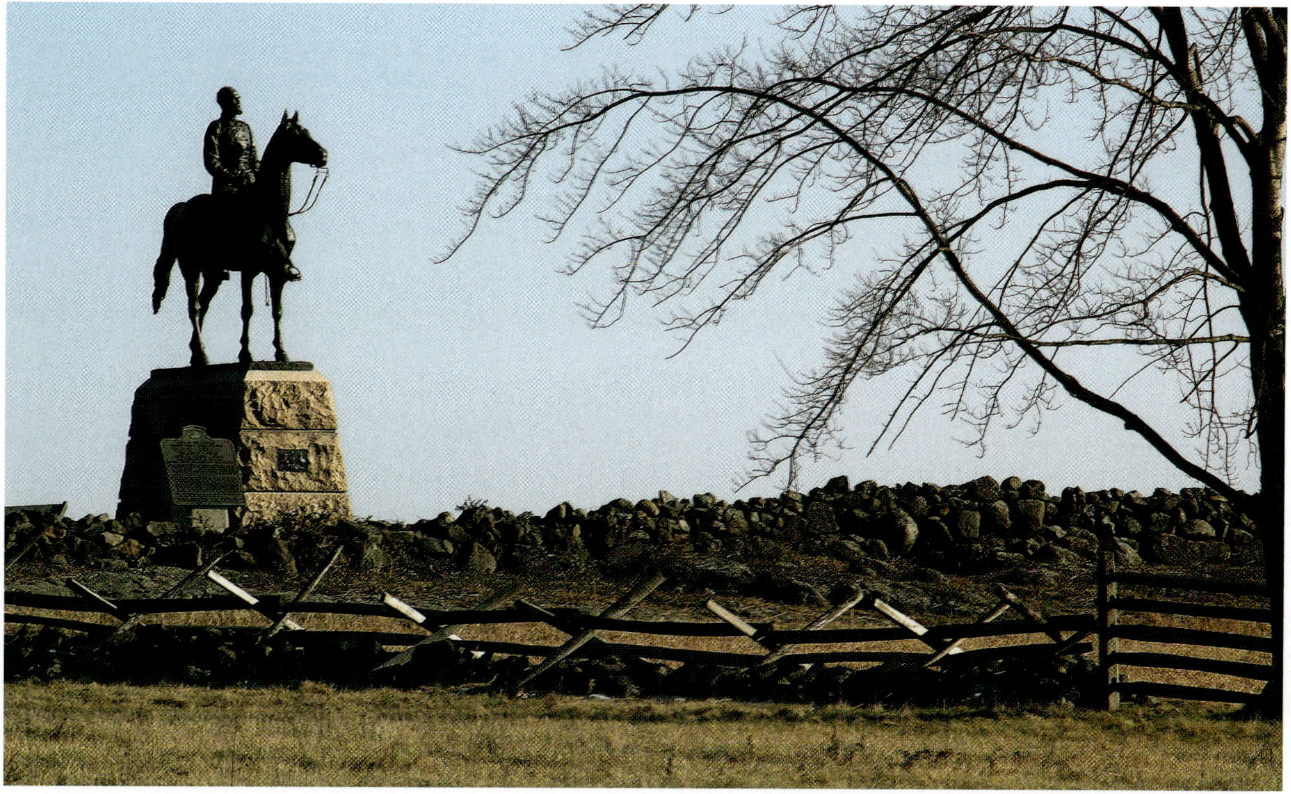

Elizabeth Thorn Monument in Evergreen Cemetery

"It was a busy time for father and me when we got back. We would get orders to dig graves and father and I dug 105 graves for soldiers in the next three weeks. When I left home the first time I had put on a heavier dress than usual and when we got back there wasn't a single piece of our clothing left. I lived in that dress for six weeks."

Elizabeth Thorn
Gettysburg civilian
Quoted in *Firestorm at Gettysburg: Civilian Voices* by Jim Slade & John Alexander, p. 146.

German immigrants Elizabeth and Peter Thorn were caretakers of Evergreen Cemetery. At the time of the battle, Peter was away with his regiment and Elizabeth, who was six months pregnant, was at home, taking care of her elderly parents as well as her own three small children. After the battle, Elizabeth oversaw the burials of many of the Union soldiers and dug quite a few of the graves herself. Three months after the battle, her daughter Rosie Meade Thorn was born.

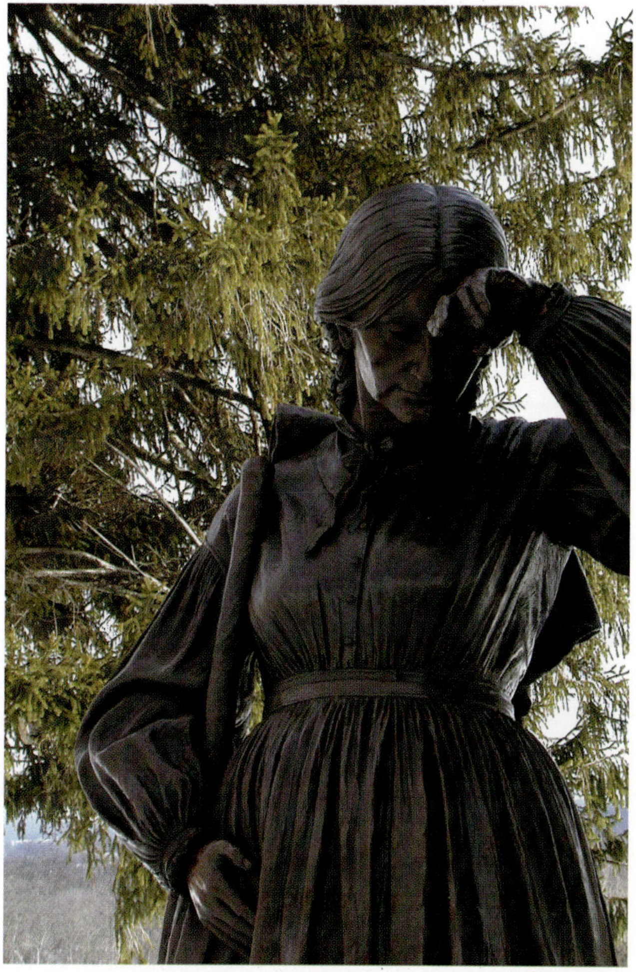

Top of Pennsylvania Memorial

Lo, Victress on the peaks,
Where thou, with mighty brow regarding the world,
(The world, O Libertad, that vainly conspired against thee),
Out of its countless beleaguering toils, after thwarting them all,
Dominant, with the dazzling sun around thee,
Flauntest now unharm'd in immortal soundness and bloom - lo, in these hours supreme,
No poem proud, I chanting bring to thee, no mastery's rapturous verse,
But a cluster containing night's darkness and blood-dripping wounds,
And psalms of the dead.

Walt Whitman
Civil war poet & nurse

This glorious statue is the winged goddess of victory atop the Pennsylvania Memorial.

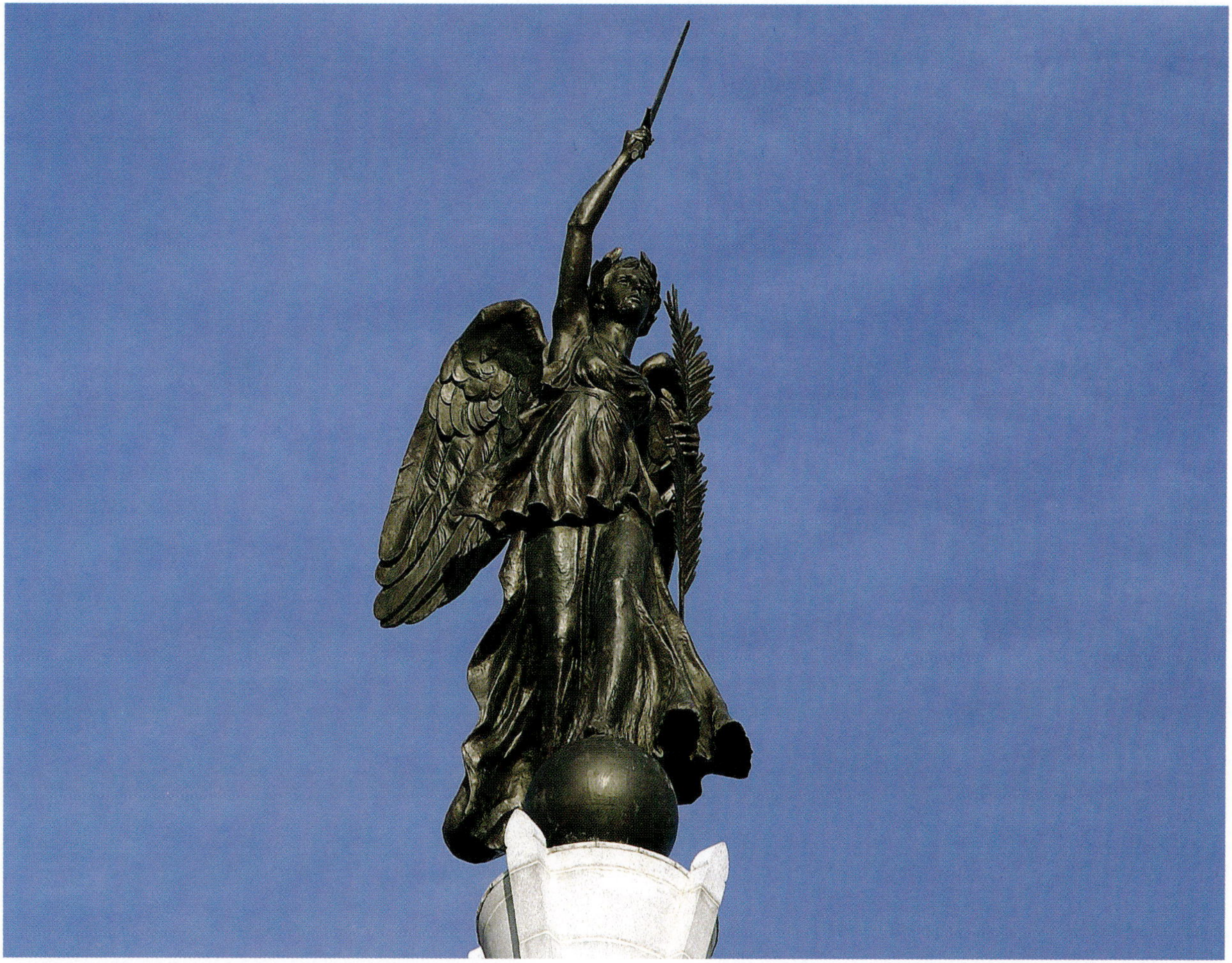

The Pennsylvania Memorial

"You are Wisconsin, Indiana, Michigan and New York boys and maybe you don't know how a Pennsylvanian feels when he may have to fight tomorrow in his mother's dooryard!"

Unknown Sergeant
First Pennsylvania Light Artillery
Quoted in *Morning at Willoughby Run: July 1, 1863* by Richard S. Shue, p. 53.

The largest memorial on the battlefield, the Pennsylvania Memorial rises majestically against the sky. The large bronze tablets around the base list every Pennsylvania regiment and soldier who fought at Gettysburg, defending his home state.

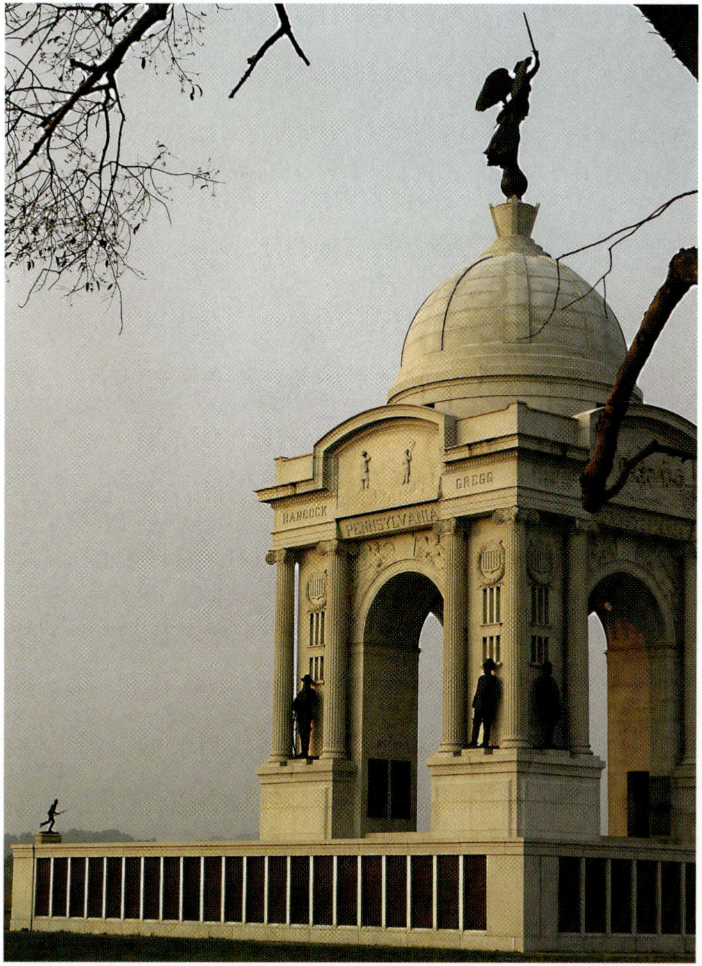
HANCOCK
GREGG
PENNSYLVANIA

Confederate Brass Napoleon Guns on Seminary Ridge

"Never will I forget those scenes and sounds. The earth seems unsteady beneath this furious cannonade, and the air might be said to be agitated by the wings of death."

Lieutenant John Dooley
1st Virginia Infantry
Quoted in *Gettysburg: A Testing of Courage* by Noah Andre Trudeau, p. 464.

At 1:07 pm on July 3, 1863, the Confederate batteries along Seminary Ridge erupted in flame and hurled fiery death toward the Federals holding Cemetery Ridge. The largest concentration of fire was aimed at the center of the Union line in an effort to soften up the forces there in anticipation of the Confederate infantry assault, now known as Pickett's Charge. The cannonade lasted for over an hour. At approximately 2:40 pm, Pickett's troops stepped off toward Cemetery Ridge and the bloody fate that awaited them.

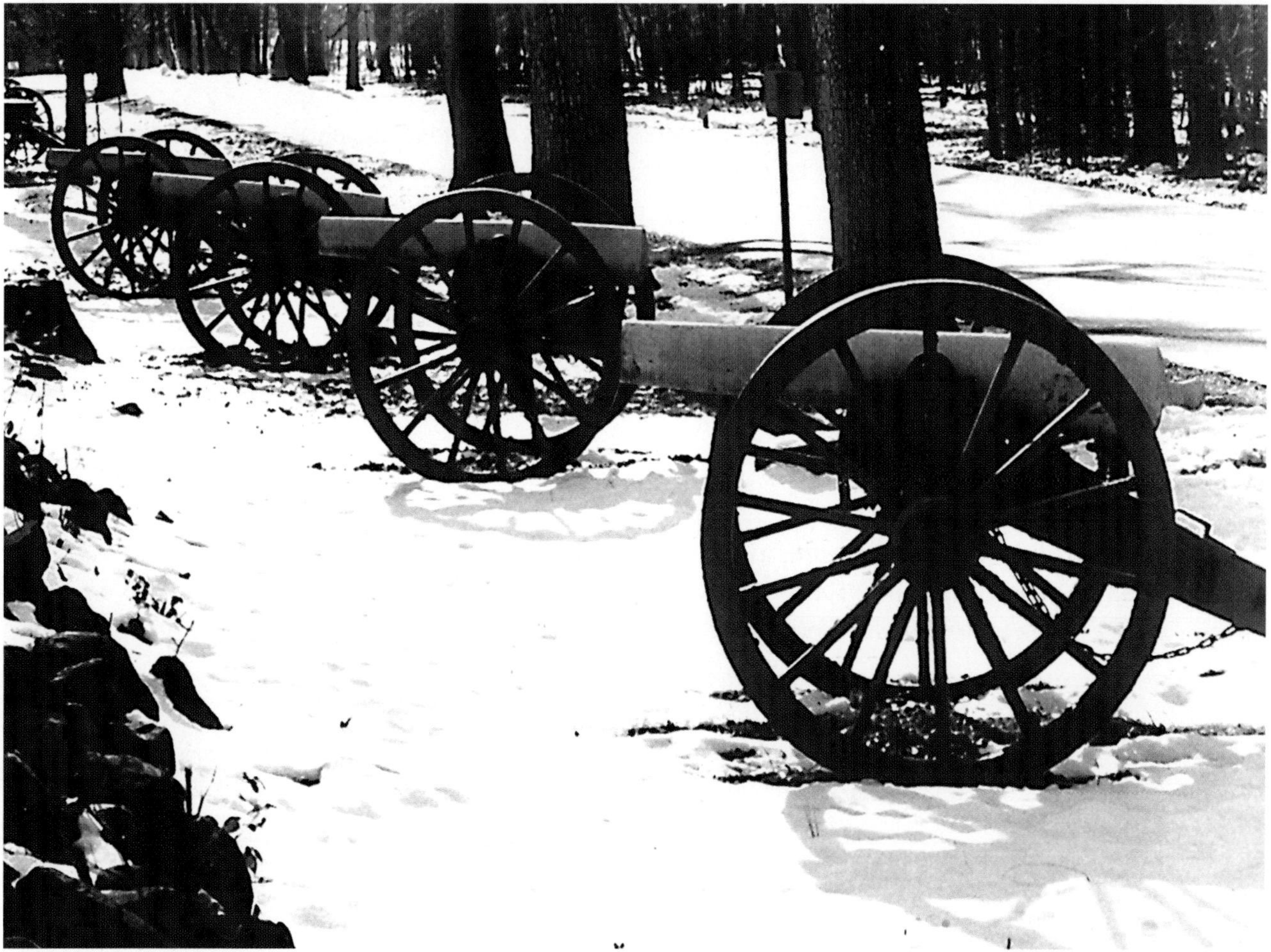

Gouveneur K. Warren on Little Round Top

"...I requested the captain...fire a shot into these woods. He did so, and as the shot went whistling through the air the sound of it reached the enemy's troops and caused everyone to look in the direction of it. This motion revealed to me the glistening of gun barrels and bayonets of the enemy's line of battle, already formed and far outflanking the position of any of our troops..."
Brigadier General Gouveneur K. Warren
July 2, 1863
Quoted in *Attack and Defense of Little Round Top: Gettysburg, July 2, 1863* by Oliver Willcox Norton, pp. 131.

On the afternoon of July 2, 1863, Warren, as chief engineer of the Army of the Potomac, surveyed the Union line on Cemetery Ridge. Reaching Little Round Top, he immediately recognized that the hill was "the key of the whole (Union) position." Troops were dispatched to defend the hill and the Confederate flanking movement was repulsed.

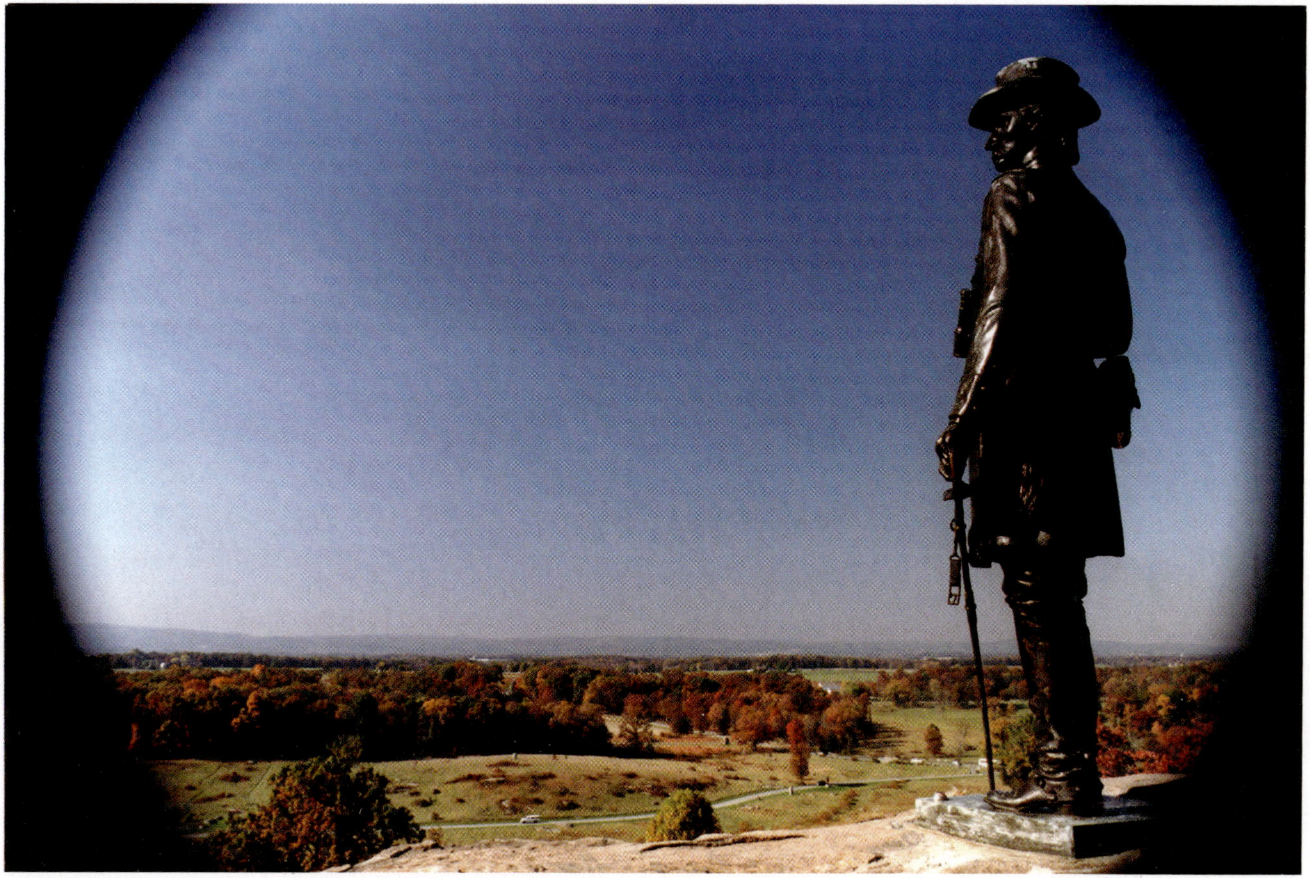

Farnsworth Field

"General Farnsworth, well, somebody can charge…"

Brigadier General H. Judson Kilpatrick to General Elon John Farnsworth
July 3, 1863
Quoted in *Gettysburg: A Testing of Courage* by Noah Andre Trudeau, p. 518.

On the steamy afternoon of July 3, 1863, after the bloody repulse of Pickett's Charge, General Kilpatrick's 3rd Division of the Union Cavalry Corps was tasked with defending the Union left against a possible counterattack. General Kilpatrick chose General Elon Farnsworth's 1st Brigade to charge the Confederate right flank. After surveying the ground and the Rebel troops entrenched behind stone walls, General Farnsworth protested to General Kilpatrick that there was not "the slightest chance for a successful charge." After impugning General Farnsworth's courage, General Kilpatrick insisted the charge be made. General Farnsworth led two battalions of the 1st Vermont Calvary against Evander Laws' hardened Alabama and Texas regiments. General Farnsworth's troops were brutally repulsed and Farnsworth himself was killed.

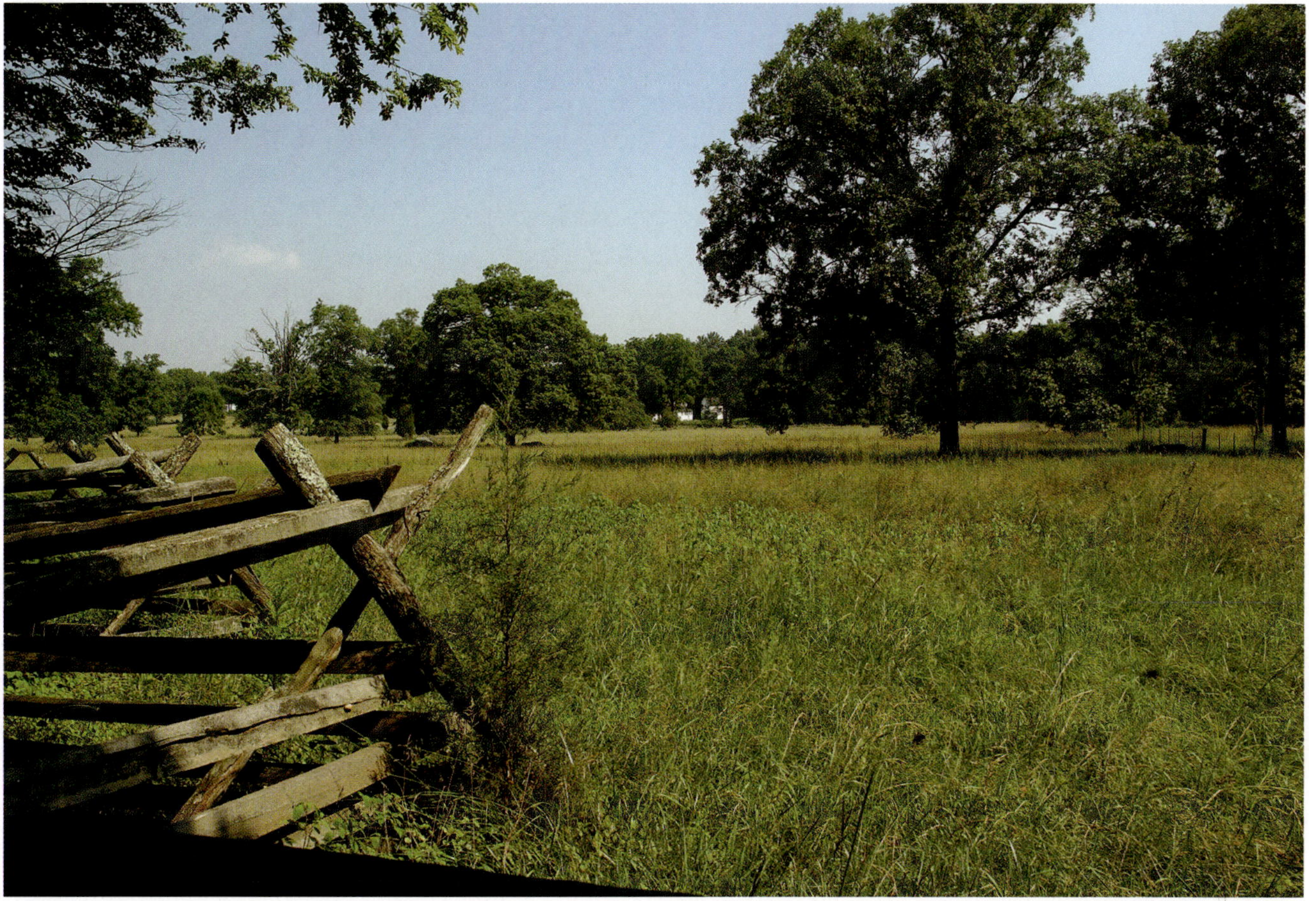

The Peach Orchard

"No friendly supports of any kind, were in sight but Johnnie Rebs in great numbers. Bullets were coming into our midst from many directions and a Confederate battery added to our difficulties."

Captain John Bigelow
9th Independent Battery, Massachusetts Light Artillery
Quoted in *The Peach Orchard: Gettysburg, July 2, 1863* by John Bigelow, pp. 55-56.

On July 2, 1863, Union General Daniel Sickles moved his brigade from Cemetery Ridge to a position along the Emmitsburg Road, a line which he considered more advantageous for battle. His troops were driven back, with terrible casualties, from the Peach Orchard, through the Wheatfield and Devil's Den, back to Cemetery Ridge where General Meade had ordered him in the first place. General Sickles lost his leg in the battle and was awarded the Medal of Honor for his services that day.

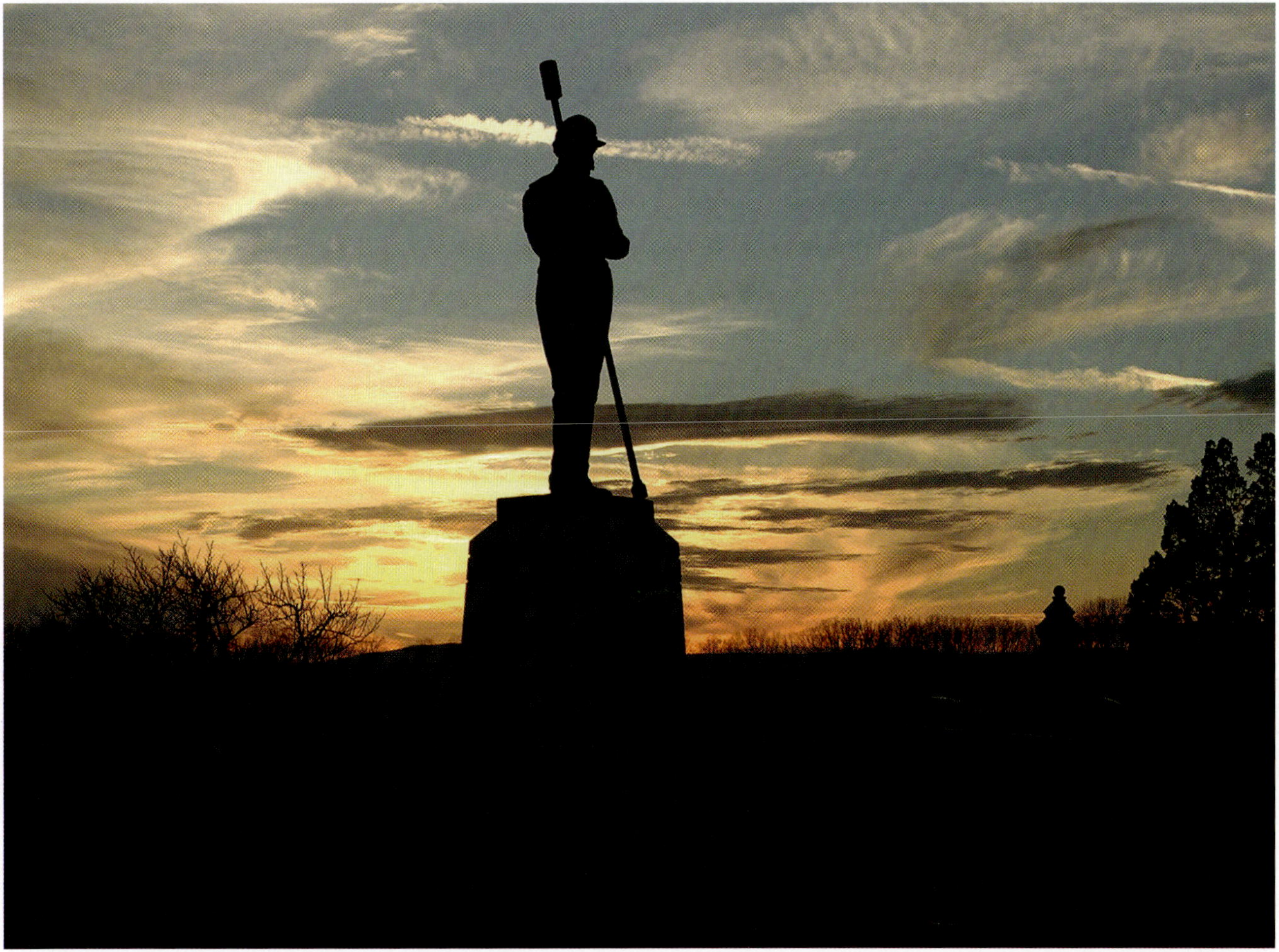

Gettysburg from North Confederate Avenue

"We felt utterly defenseless. Naturally we girls thought all the chivalry of the town took its departure in the morning and our imagination pictured the most outlandish things which would be done. Children and women went about wringing their hands, alternately bemoaning our impending fate & praying for deliverance...father hunted up an old gun, loaded it and left it in the house and then went out to hear what could be heard. Mother said, 'There is this gun ready loaded for the rebels to shoot us.' In the midst of our terror we laughed, for not one of us knew how to handle a gun."

Salome Myers
Gettysburg civilian
Quoted in *The Ties of the Past: The Gettysburg Diaries of Salome Myers Stewart 1854-1922*
by Sarah Sites Rodgers, p. 162.

Long shadows draw toward the town of Gettysburg, off in the distance. In 1863, Gettysburg was a sleepy town of 2500 inhabitants whose main industries were carriage-making and agriculture. After enduring Confederate occupation for three days, the battle was over, but nearly every home had become a hospital and dead soldiers and beasts were rotting everywhere in the hot summer sun. The residents had been plunged into a nightmare from which they would not awaken for months.

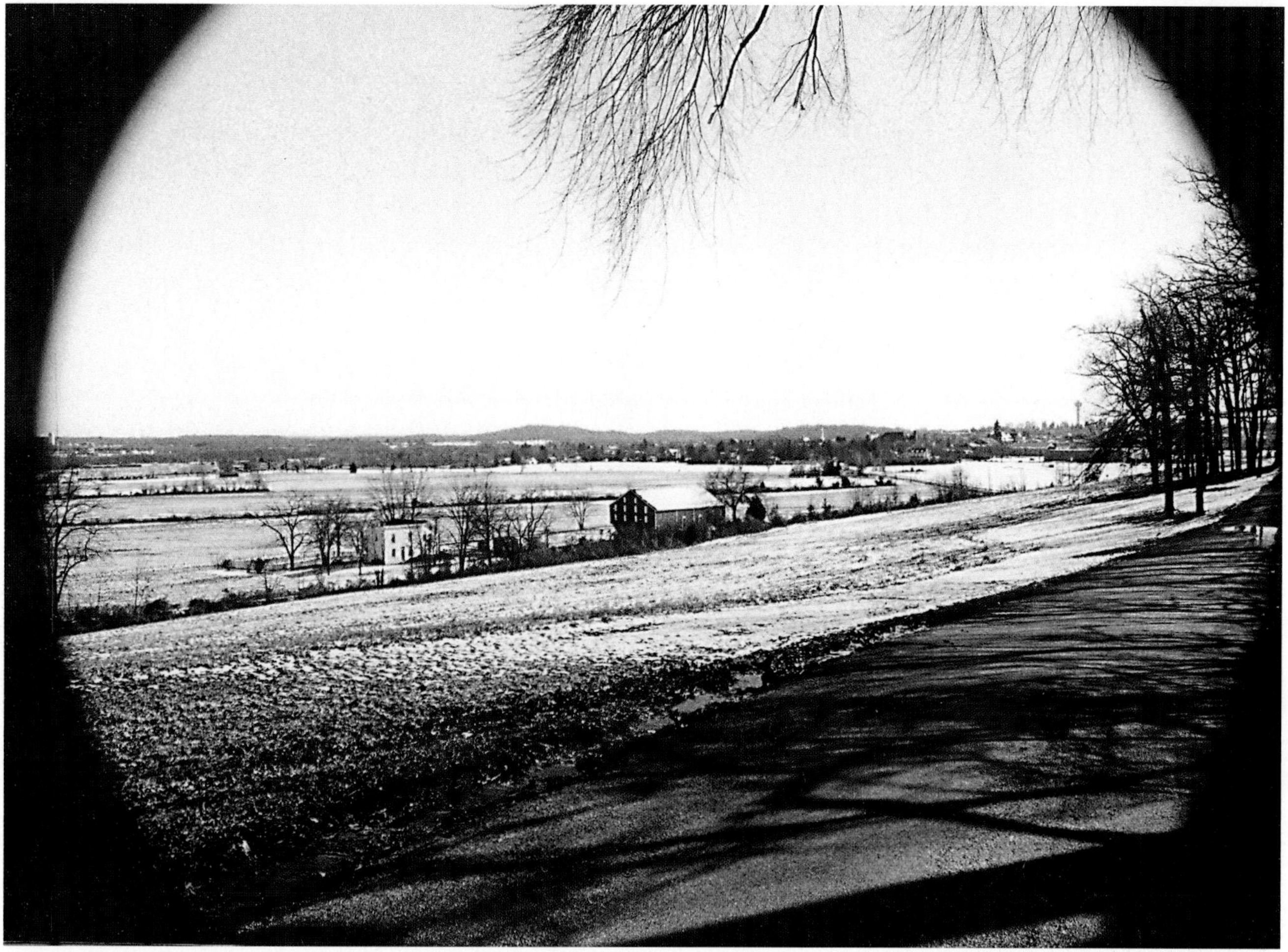

155th PA Monument

"But there is no faltering; the men stand nobly to their work. Men are dropping dead or wounded on all sides by scores and by hundreds; and the poor mutilated creatures — some with an arm dangling, some with a leg broken by a bullet — are limping and crawling towards the rear. They make no sound of complaint or pain, but are as silent as if dumb and mute. A sublime heroism seems to pervade all and the intuition that to lose that crest and all is lost. How our officers, in the work of cheering on and directing the men, are falling."

Lieutenant Frank A. Haskell
Aide-de-Camp to General John Gibbon
Quoted in *Gettysburg* by Lt. Frank A. Haskell and Col. William C Oates, p. 176.

A lonely zouave stands on the crest of Little Round Top on a soft summer's day. This monument, to the 155th Pennsylvania Volunteers, marks where the regiment held the line during the second day's battle. The 155th Pennsylvania uniform was the baggy red pants, white leggings and dark blue jacket of a zouave regiment. The original Zouaves were native Algerian tribesman of the French Army during the 1830's. They were known for their ferocious fighting and units of both sides in the Civil War emulated their uniforms.

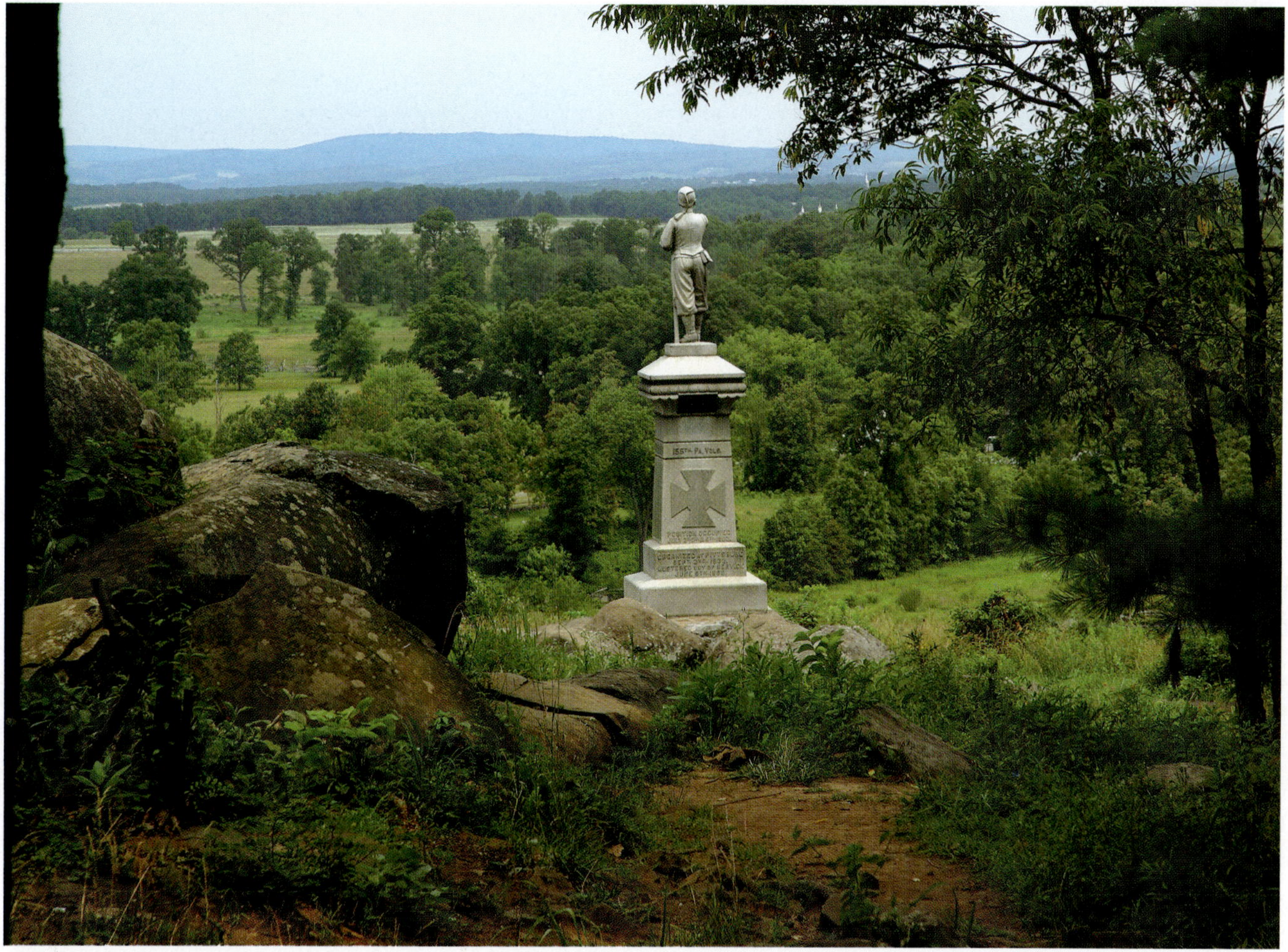
155TH PA. VOLS.

The Railroad Cut

"The men [were] black and grimy with powder and heat. They seemed all unconscious to the terrible situation, they were mad and fought with a desperation seldom witnessed."

Private Earl A. Rogers
6th Wisconsin Volunteer Infantry
Quoted in *Gettysburg: A Testing of Courage* by Noah Andre Trudeau, p. 195.

On the morning of July 1, 1863, the men of the 6th Wisconsin, 95th New York and 14th Brooklyn charged the railroad cut, which was held by Confederates of Heth's Division. The Union soldiers were decimated by the Confederates, who used the walls of the cut as cover. The Yankees persisted, however, and eventually won the approach to the cut, gaining the advantage of firing down upon the now trapped Rebels. The cost to both sides was appalling. Though Union forces gained the field for a time, by the end of the day they were driven back into town.

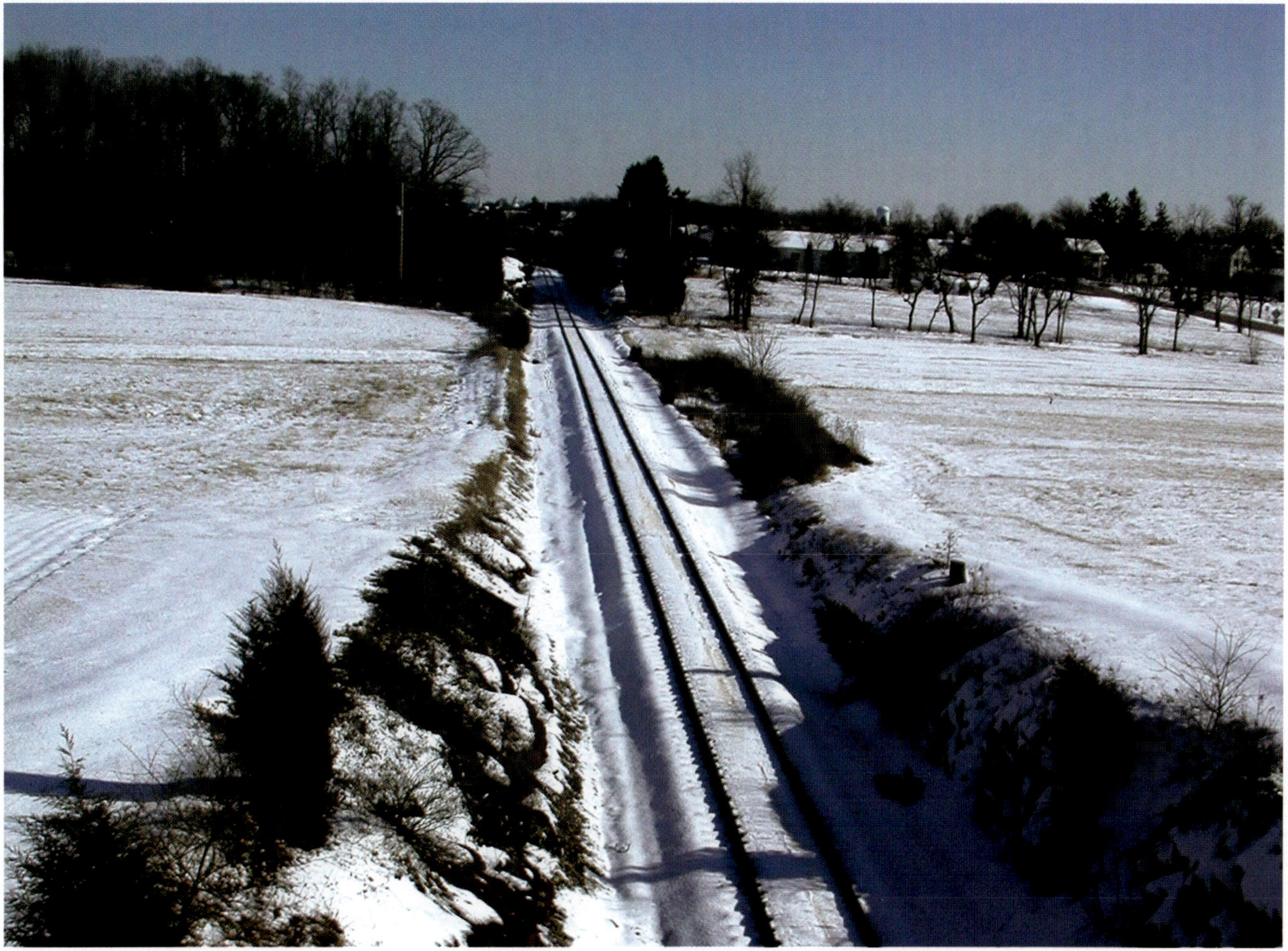

The Irish Brigade Monument

"Is that not a magnificent sight?"

A South Carolina officer, remarking at the appearance of the Irish Brigade marching into battle
Quoted in *Gettysburg: A Testing of Courage* by Noah Andre Trudeau, p. 363.

Commanded by Colonel Patrick Kelly, the Irish Brigade, consisting of the 69th, 63rd & 88th New York, the 116th Pennsylvania and the 28th Massachusetts, fought in the area of the Wheatfield. The battle raged back and forth across the field, each side temporarily gaining possession until finally the Confederates drove the Union troops back towards Devil's Den and Cemetery Ridge. The cost was high for the Irish Brigade. Beginning the fight with 532 men, 198 were killed, wounded, or missing by battle's end.

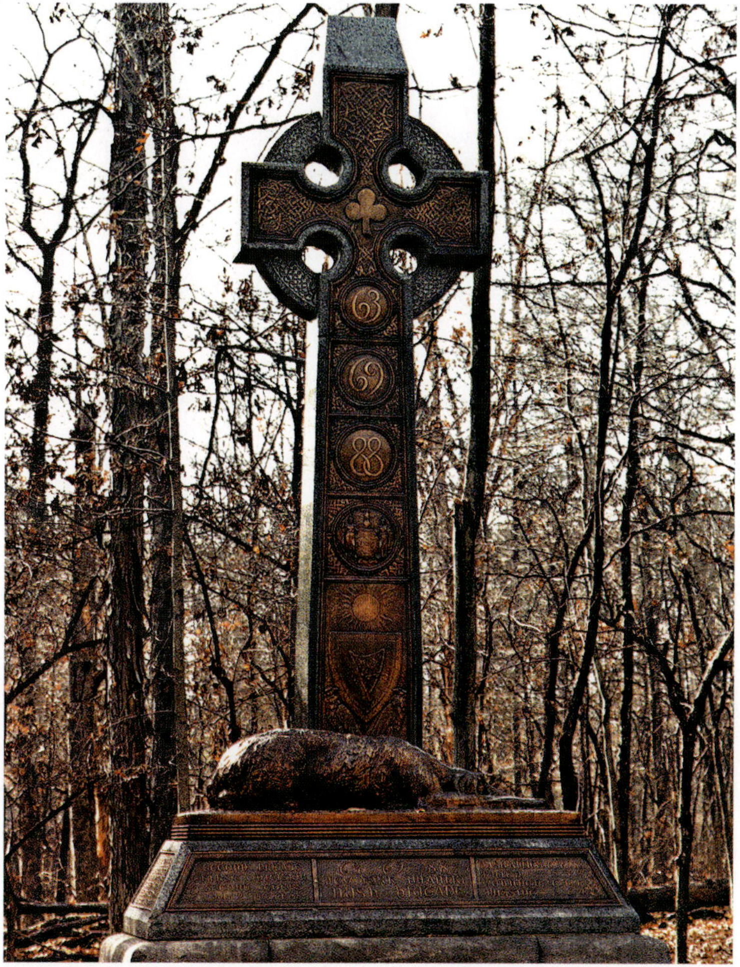
63
69
88

John Buford

"They will attack you in the morning and they will come booming — skirmishers three deep. You will have to fight like the devil to hold your own until supports arrive. The enemy must know the importance of this position and will strain every nerve to secure it, and if we are able to hold we will do well."

General John Buford to Colonel Thomas C. Devin
July 1, 1863
Quoted in *Morning at Willoughby Run: July 1, 1863* by Richard S. Shue, p. 47.

Standing strong and ever vigilant, General Buford surveys his position along the Chambersburg Pike. A veteran cavalryman, Buford is largely credited with selecting the field at Gettysburg as the perfect ground upon which to fight. Behind the Buford portrait statue, is General John F. Reynolds, commander of the Union First Corps. Despite heavy losses, Buford's men held their position until Reynolds and his troops arrived. Reynolds, however, was killed nearby in Herbst's Woods (now called Reynolds Woods) shortly after arriving at the battle.

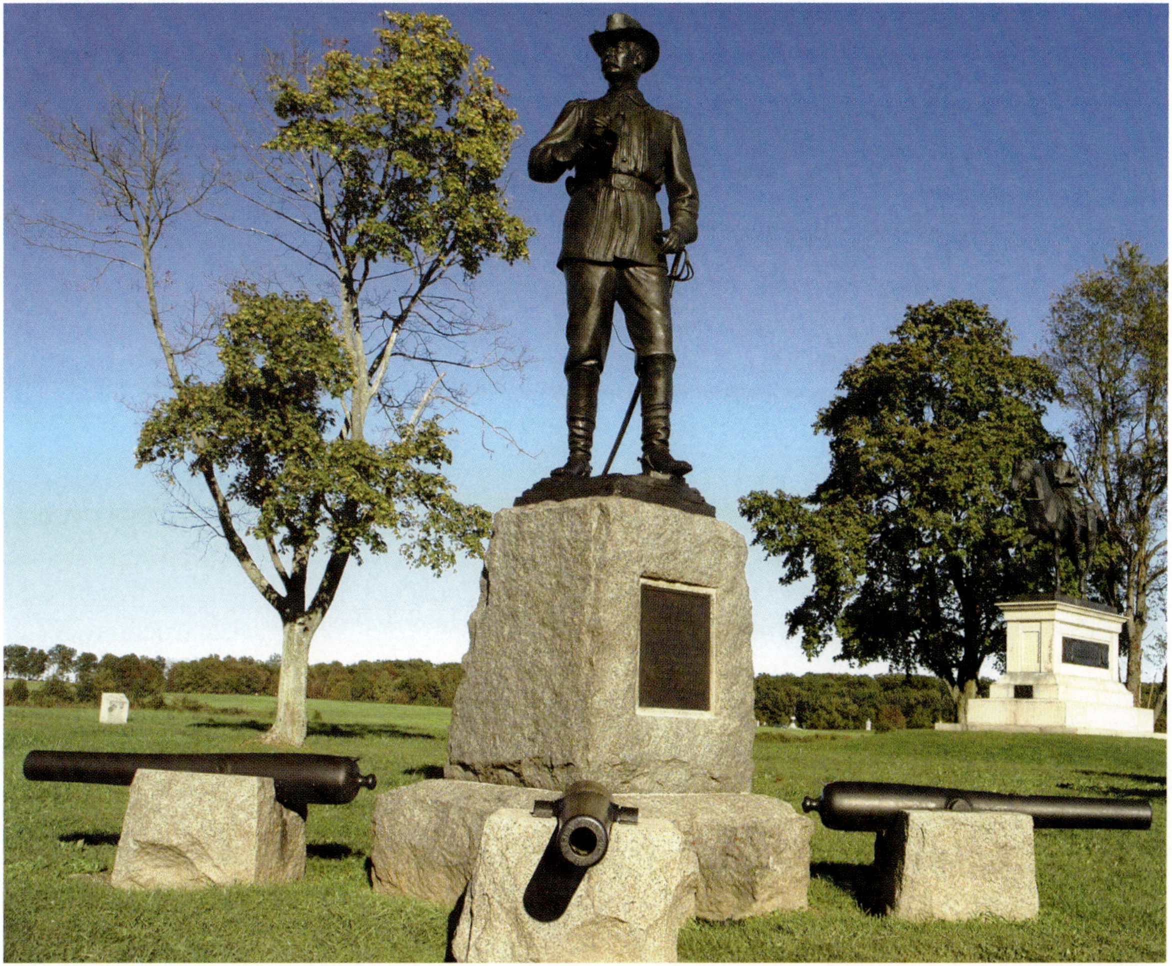

Valley of Death/Little Round Top.

"I sat there alone, on the storied crest, till the sun went down as it did before over the misty hills, and the darkness crept up the slopes, till from all earthly sight I was buried as with those before. But oh, what radiant companionship rose around, what steadfast ranks of power, what bearing of heroic souls."

Colonel Joshua L. Chamberlain
20th Maine Volunteer Infantry
Quoted in *Through Blood and Fire at Gettysburg* by General Joshua Lawrence Chamberlain, p. 28

As the late summer sun goes down, the hill of Little Round Top is ignited in a fiery orange glow. A popular spot for veterans and tourists alike to watch the brilliant Gettysburg sunsets, Little Round Top was a pivotal point of battle on July 2, 1863. The Confederates understood that if they could get their artillery up that hill, they could send enfilade fire into the Union left flank. Gen. G. K. Warren recognized the danger and sent troops to occupy the summit. The Union line held.

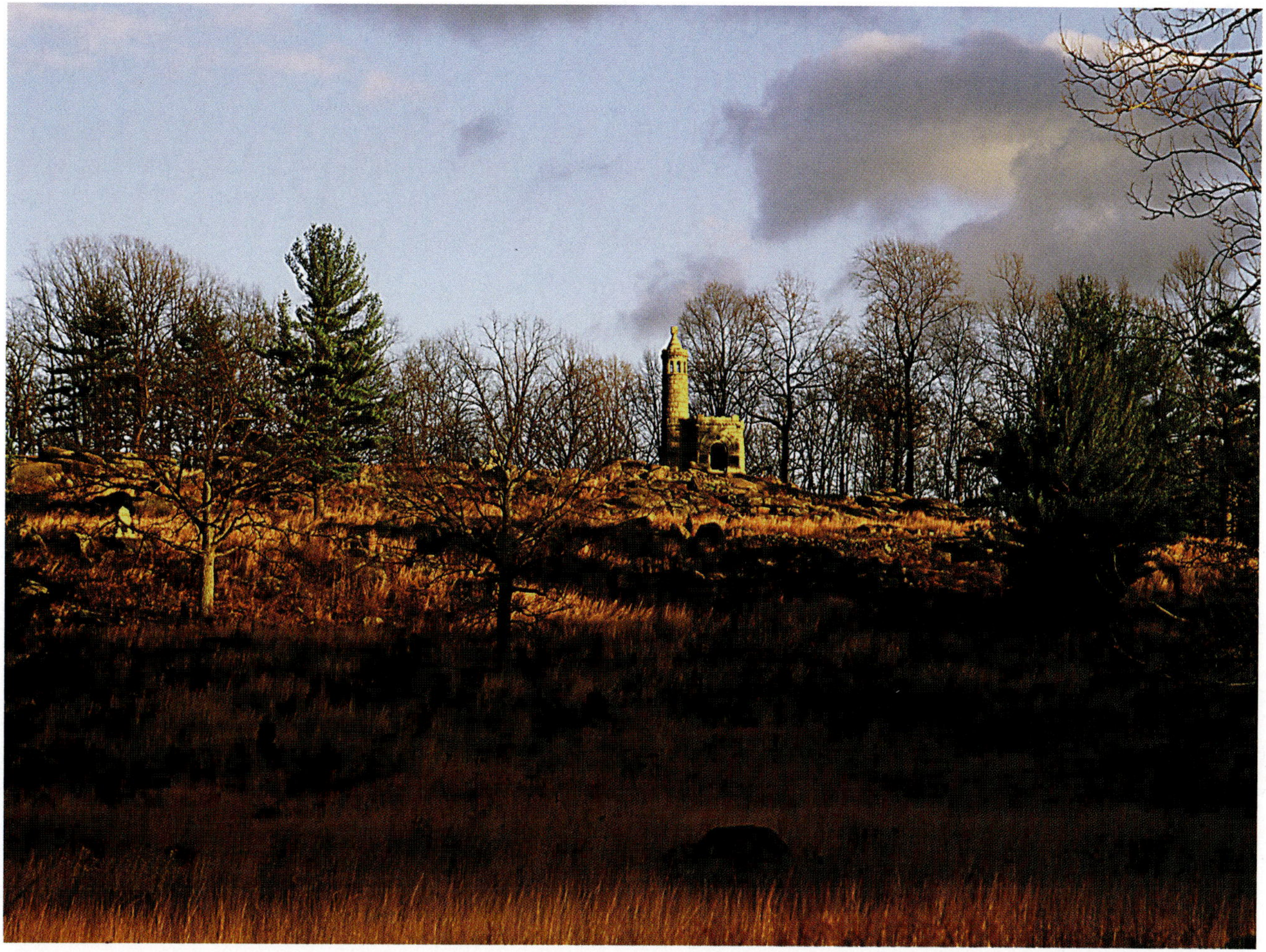

The Peace Light Memorial

"I feel that we are on the eve of a new era, when there is to be great harmony between the Federal and Confederate. I cannot stay to be a living witness to the correctness of this prophecy; but I feel it within me that it is to be so."

General Ulysses S. Grant,
before his death in 1885
Quoted in *Personal Memoirs* by U.S. Grant, p. 665.

The Peace Light Memorial shines its "enduring light" against a staggering blue sky. Located on Confederate Avenue, the memorial was dedicated by President Franklin D. Roosevelt on the 75th (and last) Reunion of the battle. On Sunday, July 3, 1938, the memorial, which had been draped in a large American flag, was uncovered by a Union veteran, a Confederate veteran and two Pennsylvania National Guardsmen. The flame on top was lit in tribute to the soldiers of both sides and as a symbol of peace between them.

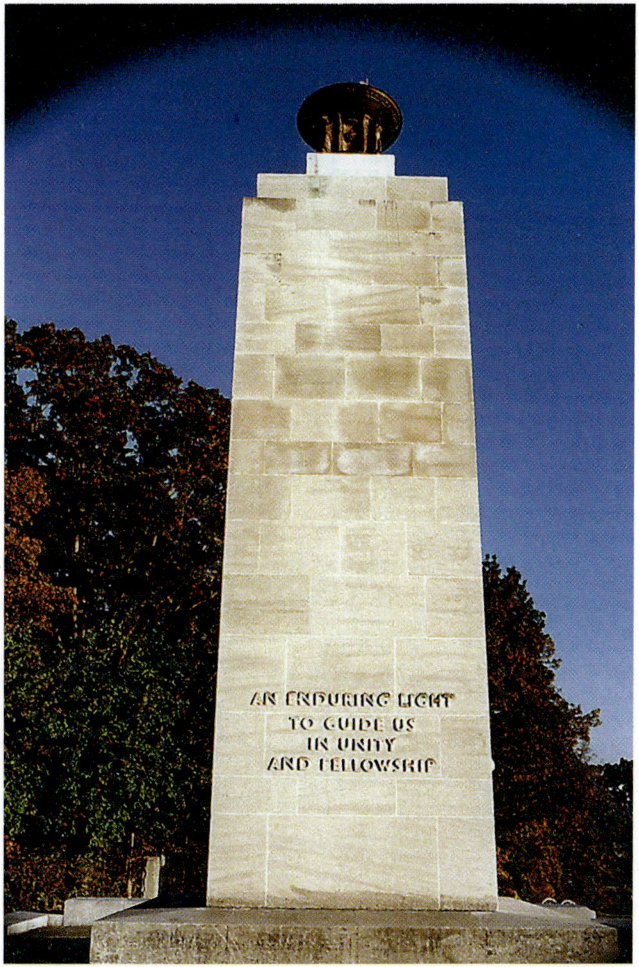
AN ENDURING LIGHT
TO GUIDE US
IN UNITY
AND FELLOWSHIP

Cushing's Battery

"That's excellent, keep that range."

Lieutenant Alonzo H. Cushing
4th U.S. Light Artillery, Battery A
July 3, 1863
Quoted in *Bachelder Papers*, Vol. III, p. 1403.

West Point graduate Alonzo Cushing's battery, consisting of six 3-inch rifles, was positioned at the Angle on July 3, 1863. In the barrage that preceded Pickett's Charge, the battery was destroyed, losing four of the six guns, and most of the men manning them. At the sight of the Confederates beginning their charge, he doggedly brought his remaining two guns to the wall. As the grim-faced Rebels marched, firing at his position, Cushing was struck in the genitals. In excruciating pain, he remained at his post, issuing orders until a Rebel bullet flew into his mouth, killing him instantly. Alonzo Cushing, one of the Union's most promising artillerists, was only twenty-two years old.

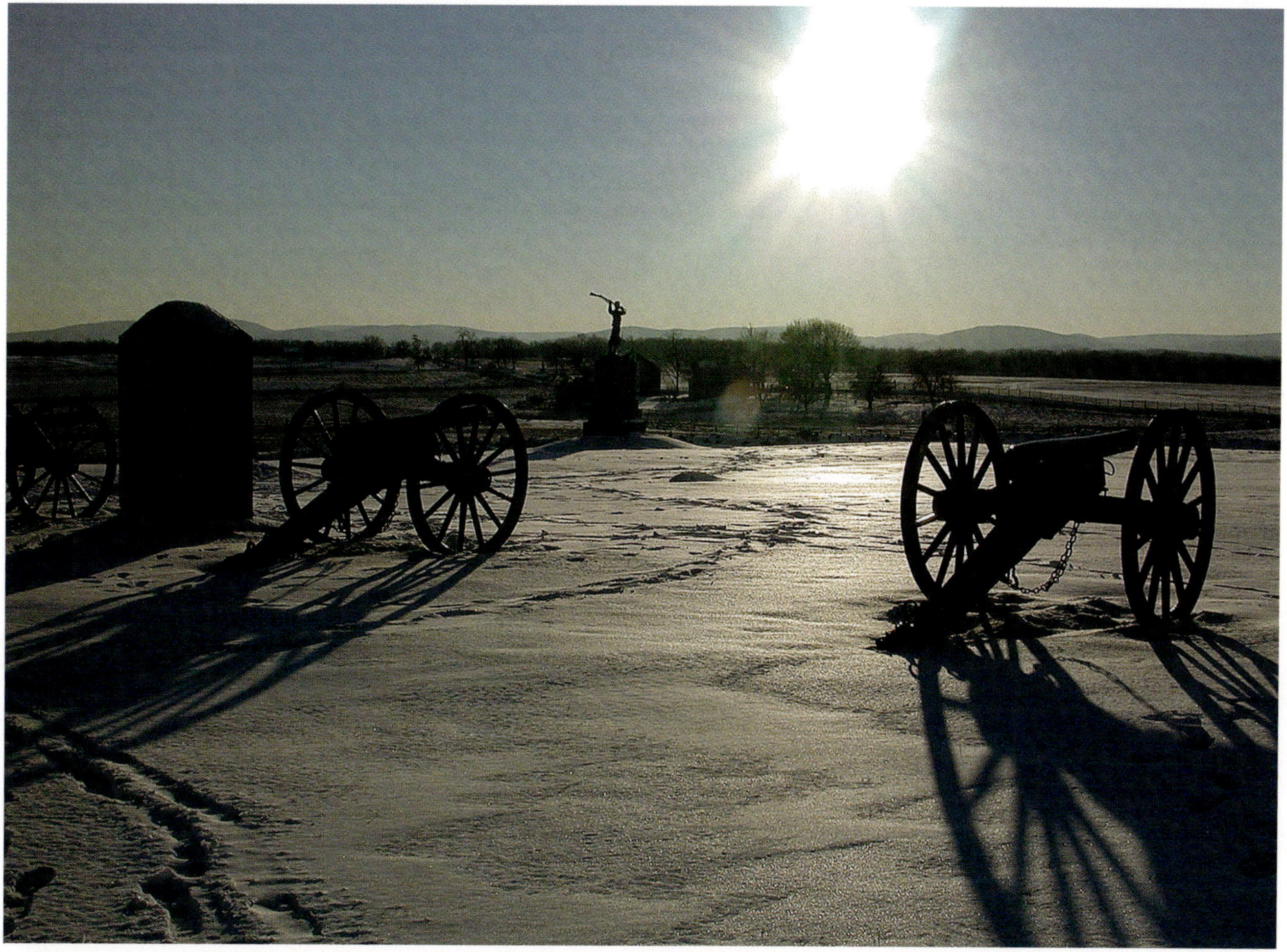

Alabama Monument

"The incessant roar of small arms, the deadly hiss of Minnie balls, the shouts of the combatants, the booming of cannon, the explosion of shells, and the crash of their fragments among the rocks, all blended together in one dread chorus whose sublimity and terror no power of expression could compass."

Colonel William F. Perry
44th Alabama Infantry
Quoted in *Devil's Den: A History and Guide* by Garry E. Adelman & Timothy H. Smith, p. 39

The men of Evander Law's Brigade, including the 44th Alabama, took part in the desperate struggles for Devil's Den and Little Round Top. Though they were successful in taking the monstrous boulders of Devil's Den, their assault was broken upon the rocky hillside of Little Round Top.

ALABAMIANS!

YOUR NAMES ARE INSCRIBED ON FAMES IMMORTAL SCROLL

BY THE ALABAMA DIVISION UNITED DAUGHTERS OF THE CONFEDERACY

UNVEILED NOVEMBER 12, 1933

The Field at Plum Run

"But, good God! Where was the First Minnesota? Our flag was carried back to the battery, and seventy men, scarce one of them unmarked by scratches and bullet holes through their clothing, are all that formed around it; the other two hundred, alas, lay bleeding under it."

"Unknown Sergeant"
1st Minnesota Volunteer Infantry
Quoted in *Pale Horse at Plum Run: The First Minnesota at Gettysburg* by Brian Leehan, p. 76.

Lying cold and pale in the fading winter light, the field at Plum Run seems to mock the bloody sacrifice it saw on the afternoon of July 2, 1863. On that dreadful day, the men of the First Minnesota held off an overwhelming assault from the Louisiana brigade of William Barksdale. The Minnesotans lost nearly two-thirds of the regiment in the encounter, but re-grouped and assisted in repulsing Pickett's Charge the next day.

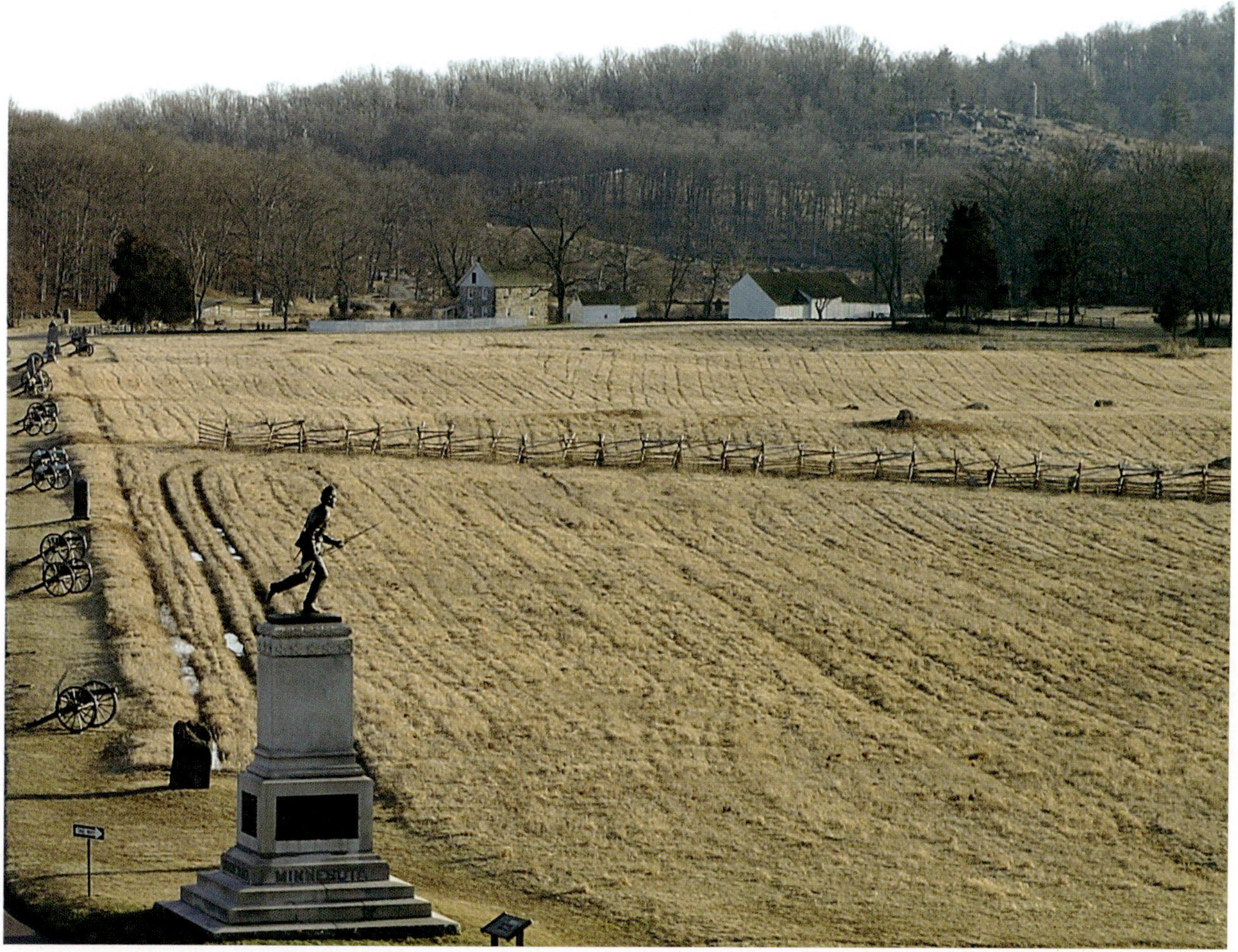
MINNESOTA

44th New York Monument

" Colonel Rice...thought it would be profitable for us to utilize these few minutes by going to the clearer space on the right of the regiment to take a look at the aspect of things in the Plum Run valley - the direction of the advance on our front...The enemy had already turned the Third Corps left, the Devil's Den was a smoking crater, the Plum Run gorge was a whirling maelstrom; one force was charging our advance batteries near the Wheat-field; the flanking force was pressing past the base of the Round Tops; all rolling toward us in tumultuous waves...Yes, brave Rice! It was well for us to see this; the better to see it through. A look into each other's eyes; without a word, we resumed our respective places."

Colonel Joshua L. Chamberlain
20th Maine Volunteer Infantry
Quoted in *Through Blood and Fire at Gettysburg* by General Joshua Lawrence Chamberlain, p. 12-13

This bucolic scene contrasts sharply from that of Colonel Chamberlain's. Gazing out from inside the 44th New York Monument on Little Round Top, across the Valley of Death toward the Devil's Den, all is quiet in the pale light of an autumn day. The 44th New York Monument stands as tribute to the heroic fighters of the state of New York. On July 2, 1863, Colonel James C. Rice, of the 44th New York, took over command of Vincent's Brigade, after the fall of its namesake, Colonel Strong Vincent. The Brigade, consisting of the 83rd Pennsylvania, 44th New York, 16th Michigan and 20th Maine, turned back the Confederate attack on the left flank of Little Round Top.

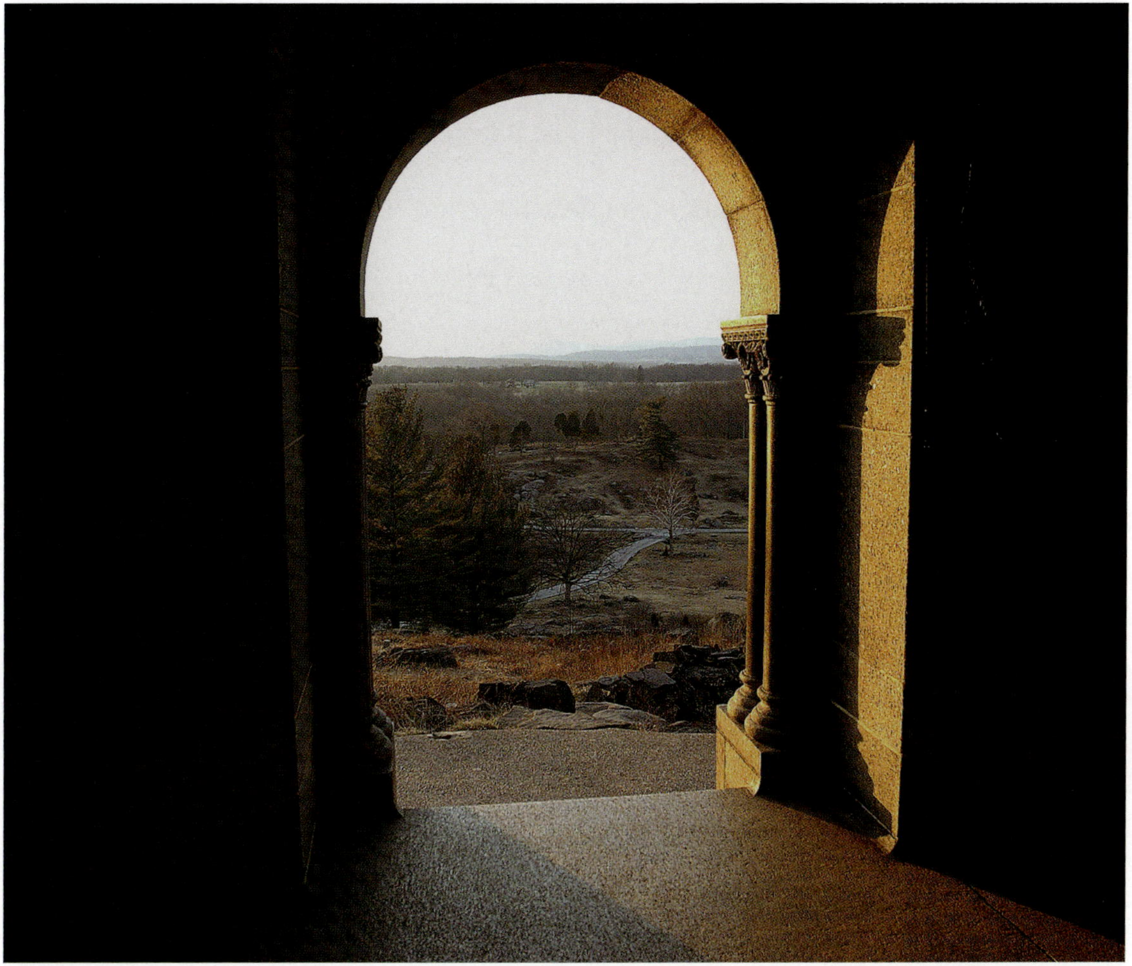

Major General John F. Reynolds

"Forward, forward men! Drive those fellows out of that [the woods]. Forward! For God's sake, forward!"

Last words of Major General John F. Reynolds
July 1, 1863
Quoted in *For God's Sake, Forward: General John F. Reynolds, USA.* by Michael A. Riley, p. 51.

As the 2nd Wisconsin surged past him into Herbst Woods (now called Reynolds Woods), General John F. Reynolds turned in his saddle to urge the 7th Wisconsin into the battle, and was struck in the back of the head by a Confederate bullet, killing him instantly. Reynolds was rumored to be a possible replacement for Joseph Hooker as Commander of the Army of the Potomac, having met with Lincoln in early June. Reynolds, however, distrusted politicians and felt that orders from Washington were interference. Command of the Army went to General George Meade. This is the spot were Reynolds fell.

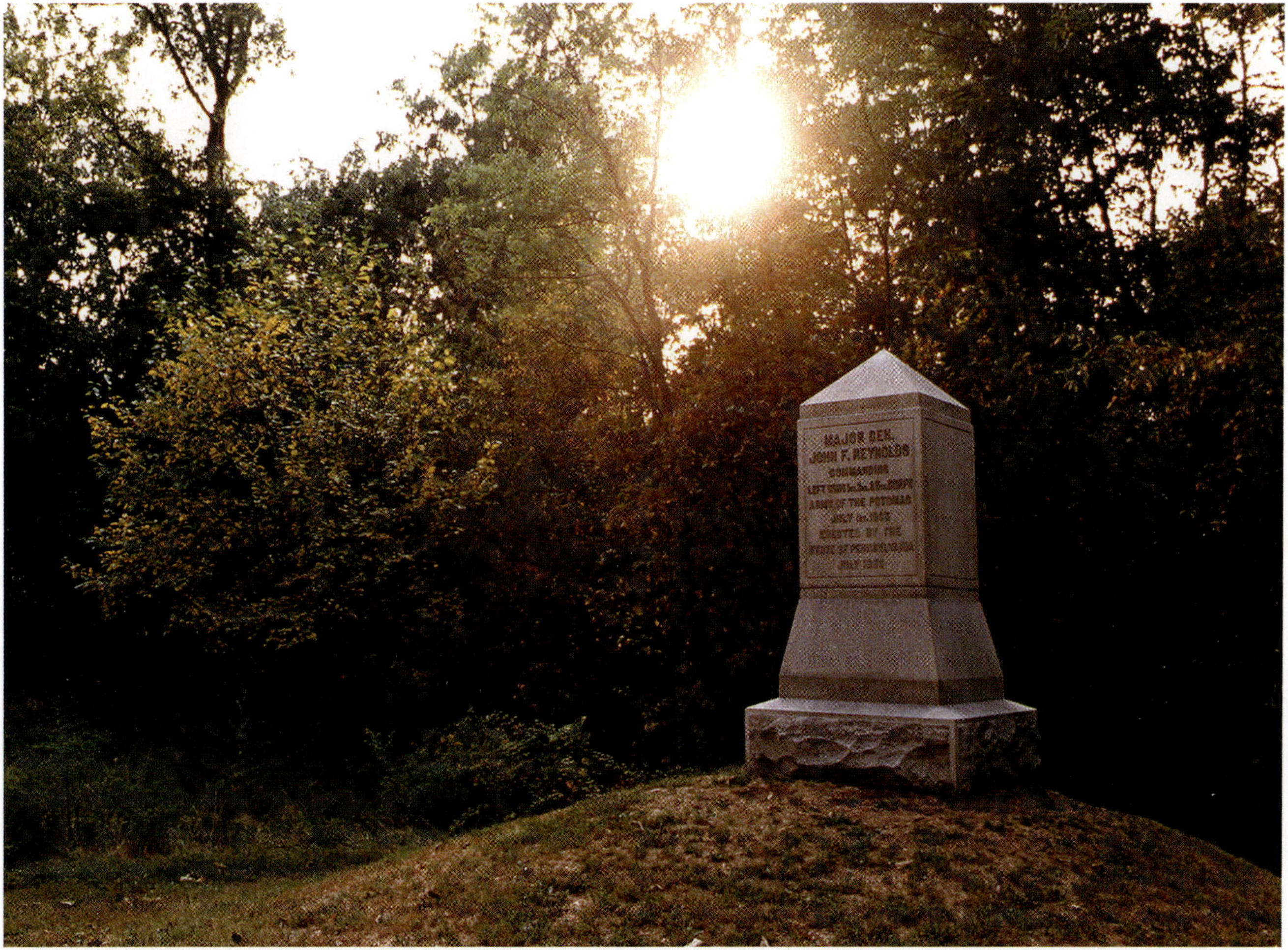
MAJOR GEN.
JOHN F. REYNOLDS
COMMANDING
ARMY OF THE POTOMAC

Position of the Sixth Corps

"General Meade said that he had been out to the front; that General Sickles had not taken the position he had directed, but had moved out from a quarter to three-quarters of a mile in advance. I asked General Meade why he had not ordered him back. He reported that it was then too late; that the enemy had opened the battle."

Major General John Sedgwick
Commander, Sixth Corps
Quoted in *Gettysburg: A Testing of Courage* by Noah Andre Trudeau, p. 378.

Etched in white, here is the position of the Sixth Corp along Sedgwick Avenue. The Sixth Corps was rushed into battle on July 2, 1863 to fill the gap created by Daniel Sickles' decision to move his troops from Cemetery Ridge to the Peach Orchard.

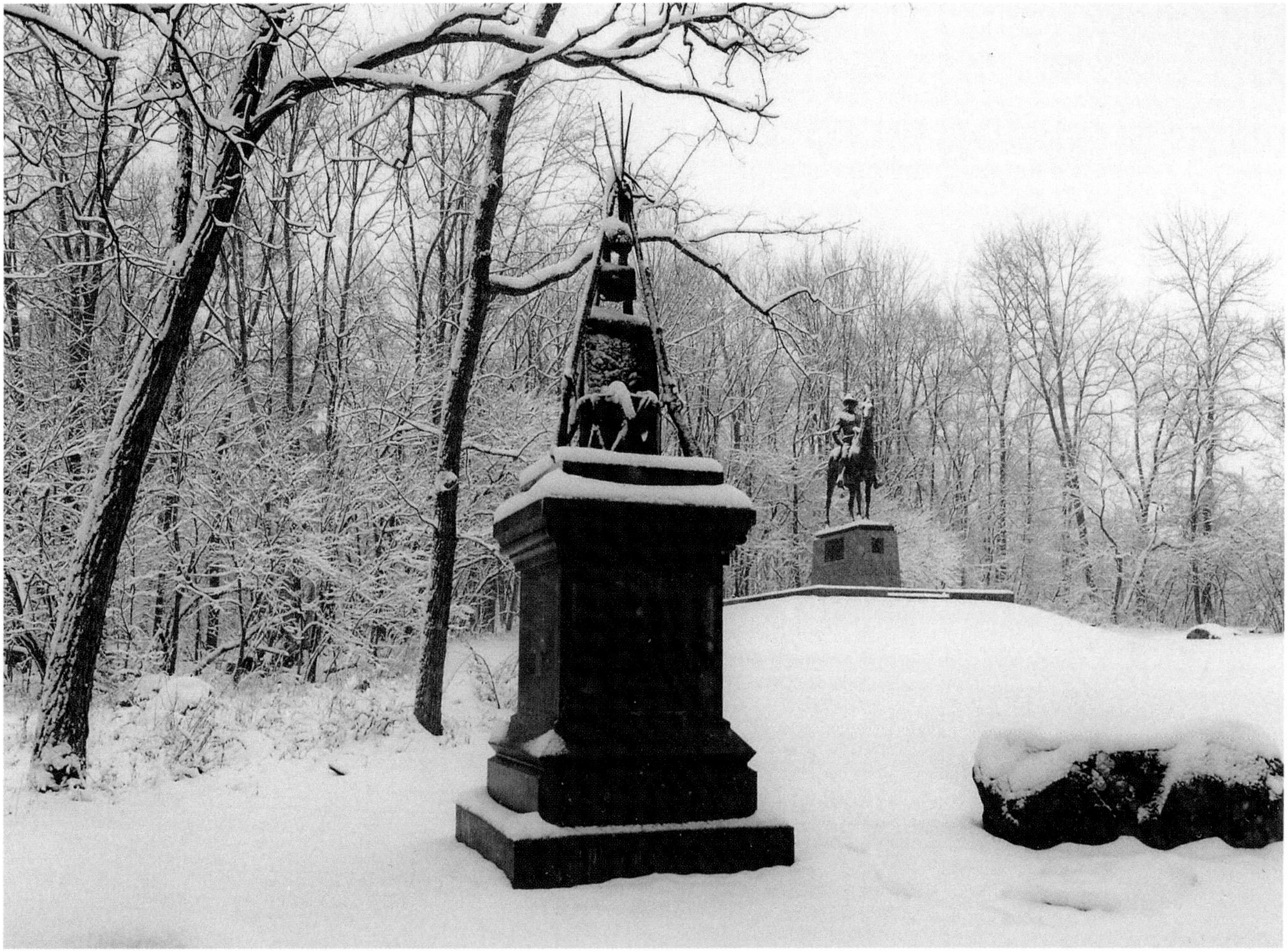

High Water Mark Memorial

"The result of the battle of Gettysburg, together with the fall of Vicksburg and Port Hudson, seems to have turned everybody's head completely, and has deluded them with the idea of the speedy and complete subjugation of the South. I was filled with astonishment to hear the people speaking in this confident manner, when one of their most prosperous states had been so recently laid under contribution as far as Harrisburg; and Washington, their capital itself, having just been saved by a fortunate turn of luck."

Lieutenant Colonel James Fremantle
Her Majesty's Coldstream Guards
Quoted in *The Fremantle Diary* by Arthur J.L. Freemantle, p.241-242.

Despite Colonel Freemantle's optimism, the days of July 1st through the 4th of 1863 marked the beginning of the end for the Confederacy. With the brutal loss at Gettysburg and the fall of Vicksburg, the Confederacy was never again able to threaten the Union's territory. The High Water Mark Memorial was designed to symbolically commemorate the point at where the tide of the Confederacy crested and began to recede. The open book lists the names of the Southern units that were part of Pickett's Charge and those Northern units who repulsed the Charge.

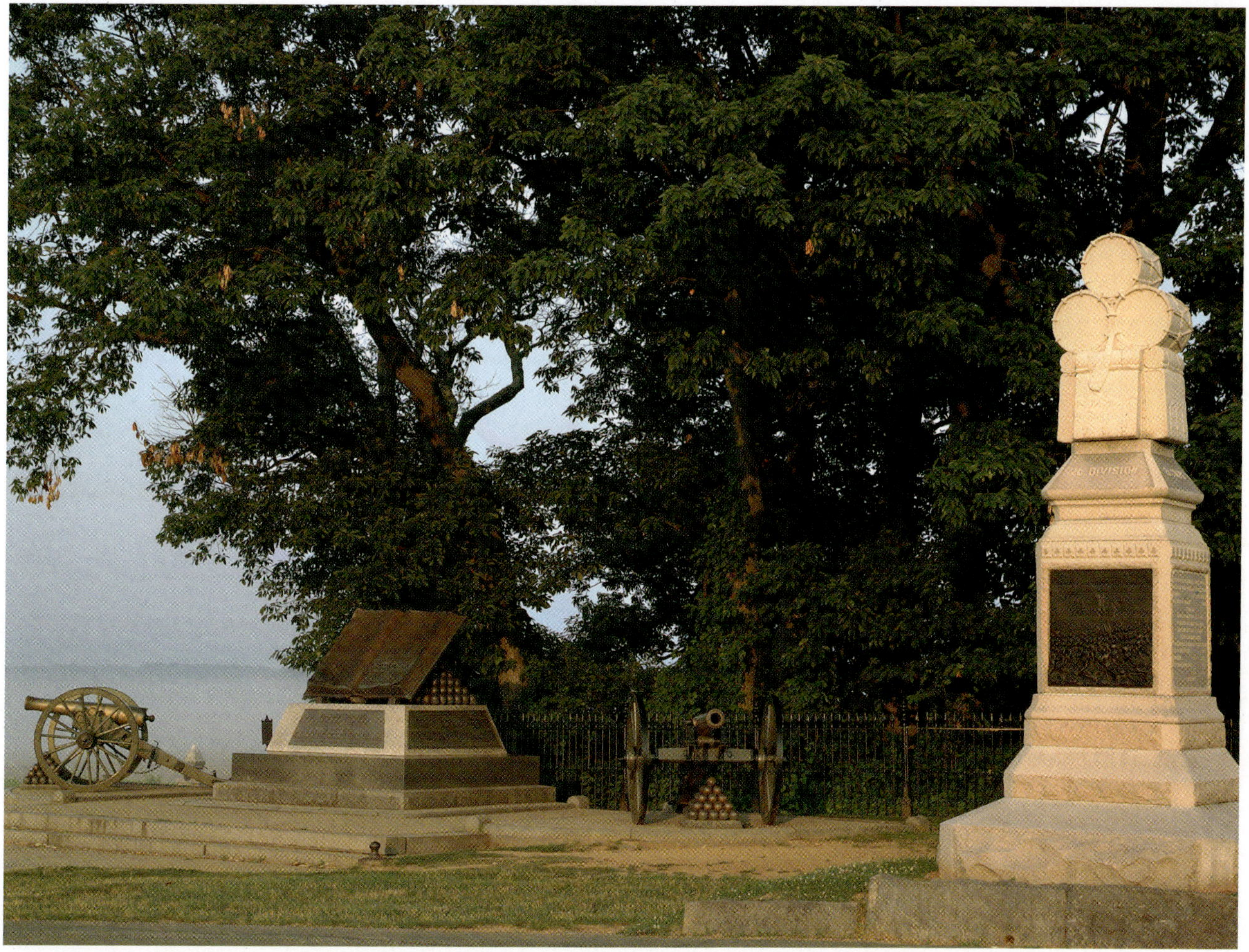
DIVISION

Abraham Lincoln

"...But, in a larger sense, we cannot dedicate — we cannot consecrate — we cannot hallow — this ground. The brave men, living and dead, who struggled here, have consecrated it, far above our poor power to add or detract. The world will little note, nor long remember what we say here, but it can never forget what they did here. It is for us the living, rather, to be dedicated here to the unfinished work which they who fought here have thus far so nobly advanced. It is rather for us to be here dedicated to the great task remaining before us — that from these honored dead we take increased devotion to that cause for which they gave the last full measure of devotion — that we here highly resolve that these dead shall not have died in vain — that this nation, under God, shall have a new birth of freedom — and that the government of the people, by the people, for the people, shall not perish from the earth."

President Abraham Lincoln
November 19, 1863

Listen to those words. Read them out loud. See the gravity of the man's face, the careworn lines creasing the nobility of his countenance. Though invited to the dedication of the National Cemetery almost as an afterthought, Abraham Lincoln, in just a few paragraphs, defined what the war — and America — was all about. His "few appropriate remarks" brought us to an awareness of what "we the people" truly means.

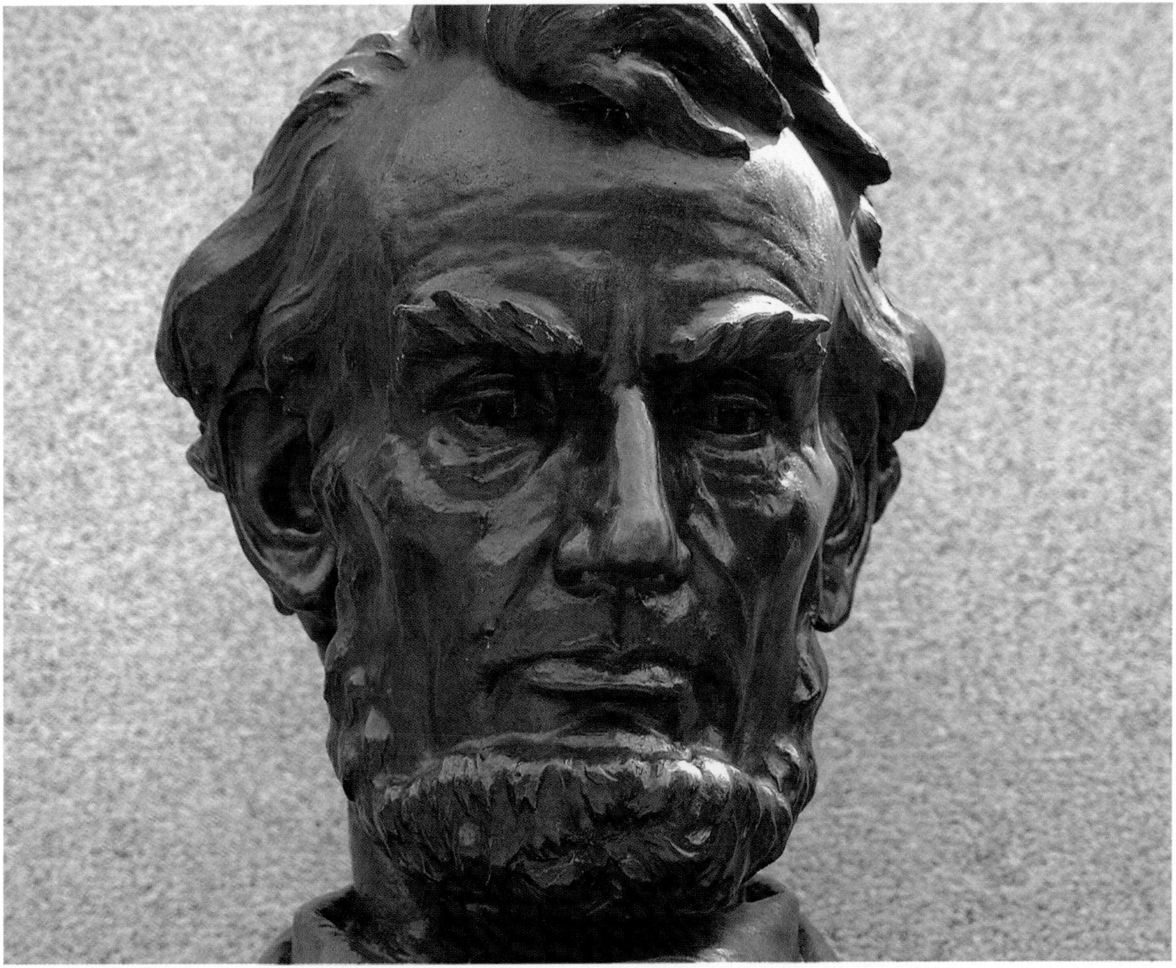

Position of the Twentieth Maine

"Our ammunition is nearly all gone, and we are using the cartridges from the boxes of our wounded comrades. A critical moment has arrived, and we can remain as we are no longer; we must advance or retreat. It must not be the latter, but how can it be the former? Colonel Chamberlain understands how it can be done. The order is given 'Fix bayonets!' and the steel shanks of the bayonets rattle upon the rifle barrels. 'Charge bayonets, charge!'"

Private Theodore Gerrish
20th Maine Volunteer Infantry
Quoted in *Army Life: A Private's Reminiscences of the Civil War* by Rev. Theodore Gerrish, pp. 109-110.

Spectral soldiers seem waiting to charge again amongst the snow — capped boulders on Vincent's Spur. Legend has it that these rocks were placed in line by the veterans of the 20th Maine to mark the position from which they charged on July 2, 1863.

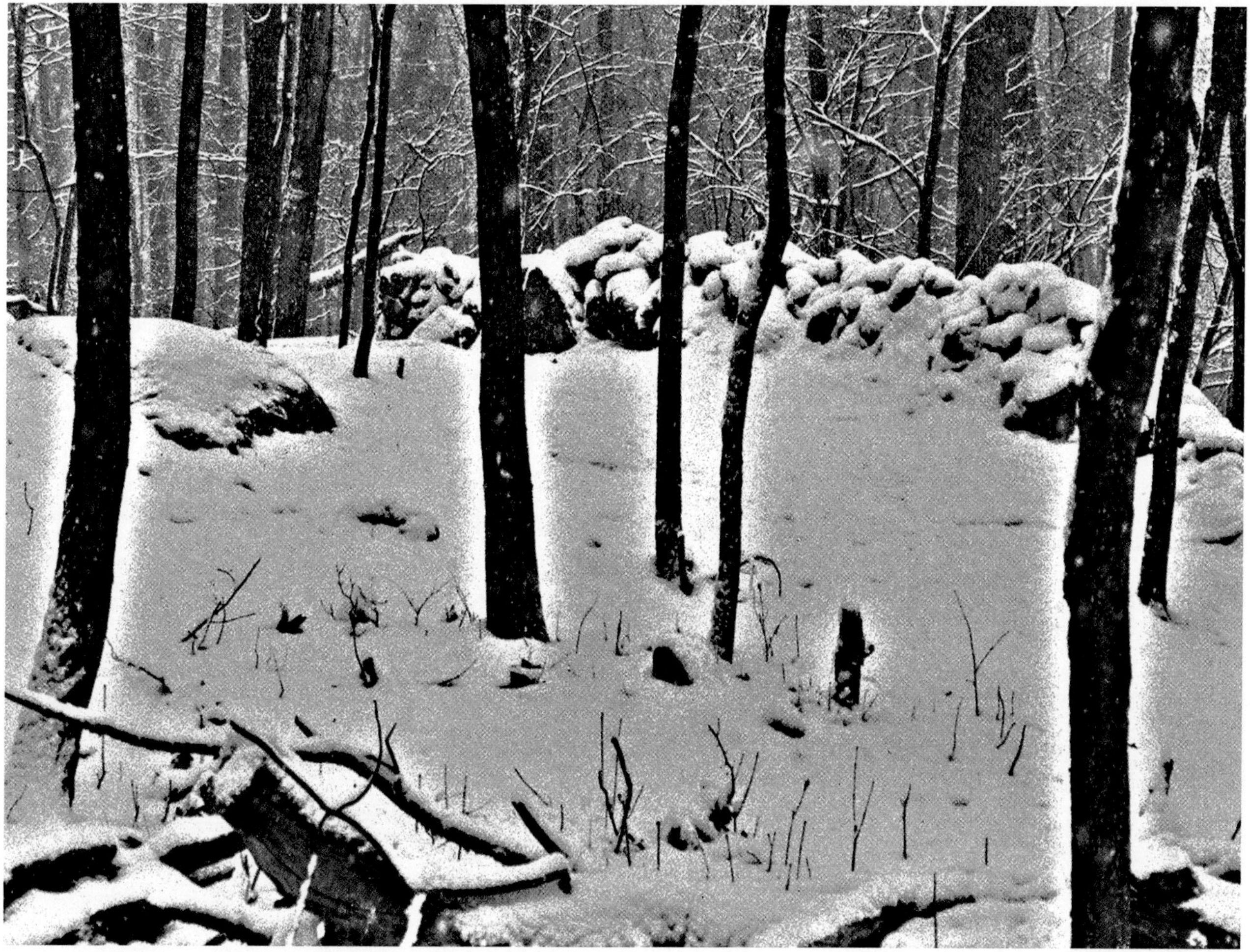

The Soldiers National Monument

"No chemistry of frost or rain, no overlaying mould of the season's recurrent life and death, can ever separate from the soil of these consecrated fields the life-blood so deeply commingled and incorporate here. Ever henceforth under the rolling suns, when these hills are touched to splendor with the morning light, or smile a farewell to the lingering day, the flush that broods upon them shall be rich with a strange and crimson tone, — not of the earth, nor yet of the sky, but mediator and hostage between the two.
"But these monuments are not to commemorate the dead alone. Death was but the divine acceptance of life freely offered by every one. Service was the central fact."

General Joshua Lawrence Chamberlain
October 3, 1889
Quoted in *Maine at Gettysburg: Report of Maine Commissioners* Prepared by the Executive Committee, pp. 558.

As you walk along the quiet tree-lined path of the Soldiers National Cemetery in Gettysburg, the sunlight beckons and in the clearing, amongst the solemn and serene graves of the fallen, rises the Soldiers National Monument. Dedicated in July 1869, it was the first monument erected on the field at Gettysburg. To the left of the Soldiers National Monument, is an urn dedicated to the First Minnesota Regiment. It was the first regimental memorial on the field, placed there in 1867 by the veterans of the decimated unit, to honor the sacrifice of their lost brothers.

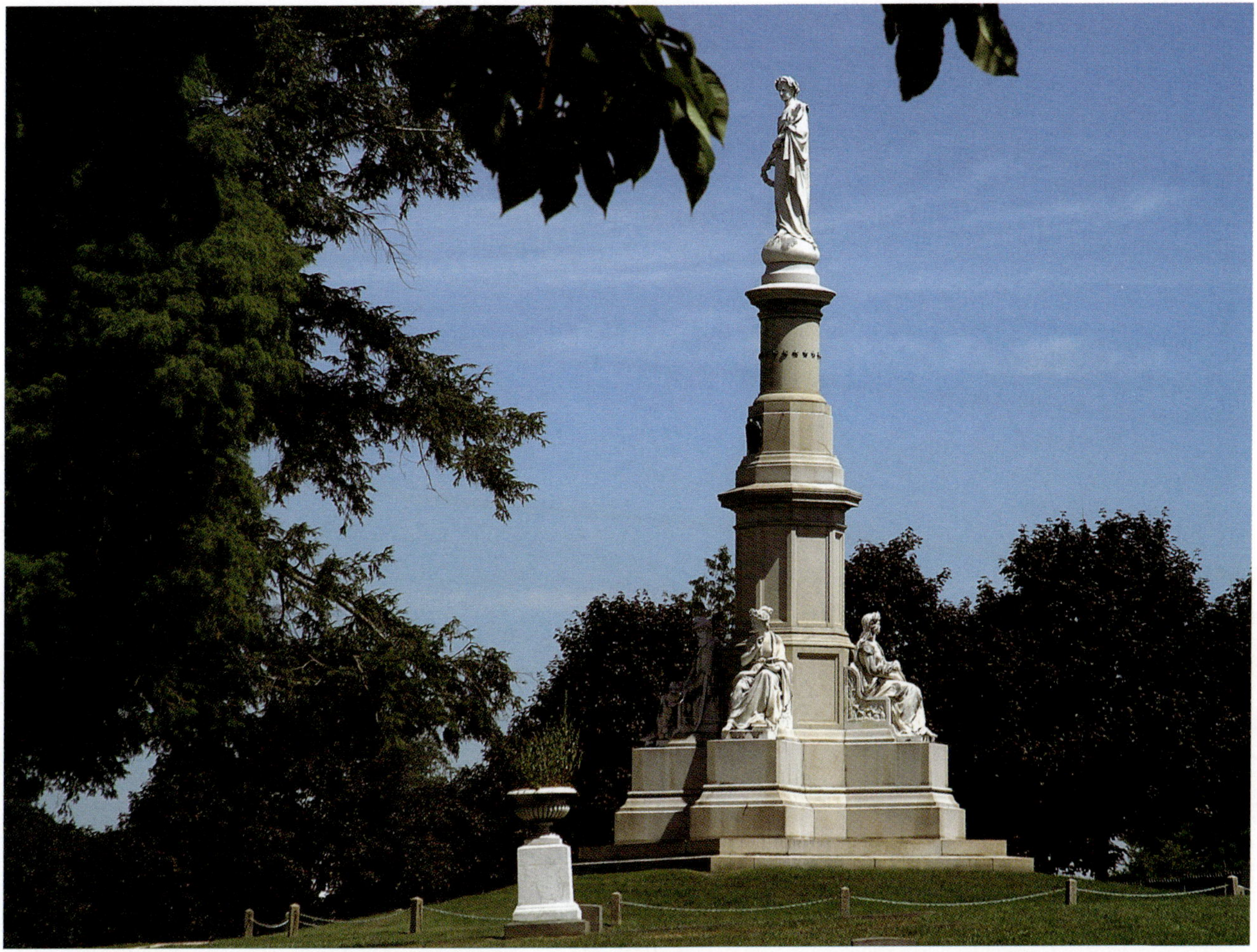

Bibliography

Adelman, Garry E. & Smith, Timothy H. Devil's Den: A History and Guide. Gettysburg, PA: Thomas Publications, 1997.

Bigelow, John. The Peach Orchard: Gettysburg, July 2, 1863. Gaithersburg, MD: Olde Soldier Books, 1987.

Bradford, Ned, ed. Battles and Leaders of the Civil War. New York: Appleton-Century-Crofts, Inc., 1956.

Chamberlain, General Joshua Lawrence. Through Blood And Fire at Gettysburg. Gettysburg, PA: Stan Clark Military Books, 1994 reprint.

Freeman, Douglas Southall. R.E. Lee: A Biography, Vol. I. Safety Harbor, FL: Simon Publications, 2001.

Fremantle, Arthur James Lyon. The Fremantle Diary. Walter Lord, editor. Short Hills, NJ: Burford Books, 1954 reprint.

Gallagher, Gary W. ed., The Second Day at Gettysburg: Essays on Confederate and Union Leadership. Kent, OH: The Kent State University Press, 1993.

Gerrish, Rev. Theodore. Army Life: A Private's Reminiscences of the Civil War. Gettysburg, PA: Stan Clark Military Books & Baltimore, MD: Butternut and Blue, 1995 reprint.

Grant, U.S. Personal Memoirs. New York: Smithmark, 1994 reprint.

Haskell, Lt. Frank A., and Oates, Col. William C. Gettysburg. New York: Bantam Books, 1992.

Hawthorne, Frederick W. Gettysburg: Stories of Men and Monuments. Gettysburg, PA: The Association of Licensed Battlefield Guides, 1988.

Ladd, David, ed. Bachelder Papers, Vols. I & III, Dayton, OH: Morningside Bookshop, 1994.

Leehan, Brian. Pale Horse at Plum Run: The First Minnesota at Gettysburg. St. Paul, MN: Minnesota Historical Society Press, 2002.

Longstreet, James. From Manassas to Appomattox: Memoirs of the Civil War in America. New York: Konecky & Konecky, 1992 reprint.

Maine at Gettysburg: Report of Maine Commissioners Prepared by the Executive Committee. Portland, ME: Lakeside Press, 1898, reprinted by Stan Clark Military Books, Gettysburg, PA, 1994.

Nevins, James H. and Styple, William B. What Death More Glorious: A Biography of General Strong Vincent. Kearney, NJ: Belle Grove Publishing, 1997.

Norton, Oliver Willcox. The Attack and Defense of Little Round Top: Gettysburg, July 2, 1863. Gettysburg, PA: Stan Clark Military Books, 1992 reprint.

Pfanz, Harry W. Gettysburg: Culp's Hill and Cemetery Hill. Chapel Hill, NC: The University of North Carolina Press, 1993.

Riley, Michael A. For God's Sake, Forward: General John F. Reynolds, USA. Gettysburg, PA: Farnsworh House Military Impressions, 1995.

Rodgers, Sarah Sites. The Ties of the Past: The Gettysburg Diaries of Salome Myers Stewart 1854-1922. Gettysburg, PA: Thomas Publications, 1996.

Shue, Richard S. Morning at Willoughby Run July 1, 1863. Gettysburg, PA: Thomas Publications, 1995.

Silliker, Ruth, ed. Rebel Yell and the Yankee Hurrah. Rockport, ME: Down East Books, 1985.

Slade, Jim & Alexander, John. Firestorm at Gettysburg: Civilian Voices. Atglen, PA: Schiffer Military/Aviation History, 1998.

Small, Major A. R. The Sixteenth Maine Regiment in the War of the Rebellion 1861-1865, Volume I. Portland, Maine, 1886. Dalton, Pete & Cyndi, ed., Union Publishing Co. reprint.

Thomas, Emory M. Robert E. Lee: A Biography. New York: W.W. Norton & Co., 1995.

Trudeau, Noah Andre. Gettysburg: A Testing of Courage. New York: Harper Collins, 2002.

Trulock, Alice Rains. In the Hands of Providence: Joshua L. Chamberlain & the American Civil War. Chapel Hill, NC: The University of North Carolina Press, 1992.

Wert, Jeffry D. Gettysburg: Day Three. New York: Simon & Schuster, 2001.

Weygant, Charles. History of the 124th New York. Celina, OH: Ironclad Publishing, 2002.

Whitman, Walt. The Civil War Poems of Walt Whitman. New York: Barnes & Noble, 1994.

Wills, Garry. Lincoln at Gettysburg: The Words That Remade America. New York: Simons & Schuster, 1992.